St. Joseph's R.C. Primary S
Mill Lane
Gilesgate
Durham
DH1 2JQ

Signposts

Assembly Themes for Years 3 to 7

Primary/Middle School
CHRIS McDONNELL

For Jenny

Acknowledgements:

To the Staff and Pupils of St Joseph's Primary School (1978–85), of Springhill Middle School (1985–88) and Fulfen Primary School (1988–), all schools in Staffordshire where the Assemblies offered here were first written.

To my daughter Rachel for the drawings.

And to Fr Gerald Coates, Parish Priest in the Diocese of Arundel and Brighton and a friend for many years, for the final nudge that resulted in this book.

First published in Great Britain in 1990 by
McCRIMMON PUBLISHING CO LTD
10–12 High Street
Great Wakering Essex SS3 0EQ]

ISBN 0 85597 443 5

© 1990 McCrimmon Publishing Co Ltd

Illustrations: Rachel McDonnell
Cover design: Nick Snode
Printed by The Wolsey Press Ltd, Ipswich

CONTENTS

Introduction to the text 6

1. The purpose of the Assembly 7
2. The Assembly as an expression of Community 9
3. The Assembly as Worship 11
4. The element of participation 13
5. The need for preparation 14
6. The immediacy of content 16
7. The circumstances of the Assembly 18
8. The Assembly presented to a wider Community 20
9. The resources for an Assembly 22
10. The purposeful use of Music 24
11. The need to be heard 26
12. The Dramatic Presentation 27
13. Texts for Assemblies 29
14. Prayers at Assemblies 30

Preface note to the sample Assemblies 33

A1. The coming of the Child 34
A2. New life at Eastertime 36
A3. Silence in a busy world 38
A4. The Child in the Temple 40
A5. Forgiveness 42
A6. Having Time 44
A7. The Road to Emmaus 46
A8. Sharing with others 48
A9. Books and the Bible 50
A10. The Bread of Life 53

A11.	Jesus welcomes the children	56
A12.	The sign of the Fish	58
A13.	Remembrance	60
A14.	Christmas	63
A15.	Having an opinion	65
A16.	Advent	68
A17.	Creation	70
A18.	Prayer	73
A19.	Good News	76
A20.	Sharing with others	79
A21.	Forgiveness	82
A22.	The wind of the Spirit	85
A23.	Lazarus	87
A24.	Water	90
A25.	Palm Sunday	92

FOREWORD

As a Parish Priest I come into contact with many teachers. What I hear from them shows me that the requirement in the New Education Act of holding a religious assembly each day has highlighted the problem of making this an effective and worthwhile experience in the child's life.

When I talked this over with Chris McDonnell, we decided that the problem is twofold. Firstly, how do you define the purpose and structure of an assembly; secondly, where you find the material?

Some teachers, with a wealth of experience, find little problem with assemblies, apart from the time needed to prepare. Others are filled with horror by what is involved.

This book aims to outline the purpose and structure of an assembly and provide a variety of themes that have already been tried and tested. It should be used as a source book, to which teachers add their own style and presentation.

The ideal would be for the staff to meet regularly to plan the assemblies for half a term and to share material and ideas. Above all, don't leave the children out! They can offer insights to which adults are quite oblivious. With the help of the children, musicians and artists a memorable assembly can be created.

Anything that can help our overstretched and under-resourced teachers has to be welcomed unreservedly.

Gerald Coates
Steyning
West Sussex

INTRODUCTION

There are numerous books available on School Assemblies. They offer many different approaches from the considered development of a theme through to the quick "quote of the day" ready made for the last minute lift from office or staff room shelf.

The intention of this contribution to that growing literature is to offer guidelines towards the understanding of the Assembly as an essential and vital element in the life of the school community. The 1988 Education Act has made considerable demands on Schools regarding a daily Act of Worship and the issues raised by that Act are giving rise to some difficulty in many schools.

It is not written with any particular age group in mind, for apart from the Sample Assemblies that are included in the second part, the discussion is about principles. These are general formulations and are adaptable to suite the needs of the particular school.

It is also intended to be a practical contribution rather than a theoretical discussion. It is rooted in real experience of Assembly in Secondary, Middle and Primary schools over a number of years in different locations, both in Voluntary Aided and Maintained Schools.

THE PREPARATION AND PRESENTATION OF THE SCHOOL ASSEMBLY

(1)
The purpose of the Assembly

(i) Why Assemble?

Before we attempt to ask any serious questions about form and detail of Assembly we must consider the reason *why* we assemble at all. Such a concern also means that we must necessarily reflect on the nature and purpose of the school.

It is too easy to suggest that the only reason for the Assembly of the School Community is because the 88 Education Act determined that a corporate Act of Worship should take place each school day. In any case, the Assembly might be considered to be broader than that concept, laudable though it is.

However, taking that as a starting point, the gathering together for Worship implies that the community shares some common thread of concern and commitment which may or may not be the case. But beyond that, there are many reasons why the gathering together of pupils and staff has a useful and essential purpose.

On the practical front, the opportunity to talk to the whole group of pupils at one time is valuable. The very 'bringing together' can serve to emphasise the shared experience that is the Community of the School. It is a chance to share in the good things experienced by that Community as a whole or by individuals within it who have for some reason or other excelled. It is a chance to encourage those who are not necessarily experiencing recognised success but are able to make a contribution to that Assembly in a particular way. It is a time for the varying aspects of school life to be noticed, be they the academic success from the classroom, some sporting achievement or a particular contribution made to the local community. It is a market place of exchange, of recognition, of praise and of reflection.

There are occasions, when the Assembly of the School Community has a different emphasis, when it is necessary for the greater good to define more clearly the edges and structures of their shared experience. Such occasions need to be handled carefully, with real consideration, if they are to be effective and productive. And above all, they should when ever possible be separated from the Assembly of shared achievement, the Assembly of Worship. Nothing is more destructive of a good Assembly, well prepared, carefully presented, than to finish on a sour note and so send everyone away with the wrong associations. Should it be necessary to speak to a large group in a corrective or reproving manner where the clear intention is to demand an improvement in behaviour, then choose another time other than the normal Assembly. Don't confuse the occasion and so set up a poor atmosphere for future Assemblies.

(ii) Groupings

We tend to regard the word 'Assembly' as applying to the whole School Community and of course, there are many occasions when such a definition is justified. But on the practical level, there are many other occasions when the identifiable groups within the overall School Community have a greater need to be together. Depending on the age range of the school (Primary, Secondary, First, Middle, High etc) so these groupings will vary. It might be that a year group of pupils meet together, or the older pupils of a Primary School, or a House group ranging from First to Fifth form level in a Secondary school. Whatever the grouping that is brought together, it will have some definable identity within the school. The pupils (and staff) will therefore come to that Assembly with a common purpose.

Even the smallest recognisable group within a school, the class group, can fruitfully 'assemble' together if care is taken to create a situation that is different from the normal gathering for registration. Such assembly can be a valuable contribution to the cohesive identity of a class, giving a sense of loyalty and purpose which can extend well beyond the immediate confines of the class group.

(iii) Staff involvement

Too often our view of Assembly has been that of staff talking to pupils; more than that, it has become staff talking at pupils. If the school is to be spoken of as a 'community' then that experience of community should embrace both adults and children alike, for both have essential contributions to make towards the success and vitality of that community.

Such a concern should therefore be reflected in the preparation and presentation of the school Assembly. We will be discussing later the emergence of Assembly themes from the curricula content of classroom activity and obviously within that context the teaching staff play an important role. But maybe we should look further than this and ask what is the role of teaching staff in the actual presentation of the Assembly, beyond playing the piano or other musical instrument, useful and important though this is.

The risk, of course, is that the Assembly becomes an occasion of competition, not for the children but for the teachers involved, each determined to produce something better. This might not be a bad motive if considered for the right 'child-centred' reasons, but if taken purely on the level of competition between staff, ultimately destructive of Assembly that is about Community. This is a risk that has to be taken if we are to consider how we might improve the experience, for hopefully the consequence of staff discussion will be a general concern to raise the quality of our communal gatherings.

(2)
The Assembly as an expression of community

(i) What is the identity of the school community?

We sometimes talk very easily about the "school community" without necessarily attempting to define exactly what it is we mean. This can lead to considerable confusion in our attempt to describe the purpose of the school and the role that each individual has to fulfil within the school.

'Community' suggests commonly held ground, both in the geographical sense – "This is our patch and we belong here" – and in the human relationship sense – "We share these views, attitudes and ideas." These two perspectives do not of course necessarily coincide. We see this all too tragically in many parts of the world where the 'community', those that share the common ground, are still fundamentally divided when it comes to questions of human relationships in whatever form they might be expressed, political, religious, ethnic etc.

The school usually draws from the geographical location of its immediate environment, although in some instances this can be so wide as to make a nonsense of any geographical identity. This is particularly the case for some Voluntary Aided Secondary schools whose intake of pupils is certainly not confined to the locality of the school grounds. But in many other instances such a physical determination of the source community of the pupils is clearly recognisable. The children will bring into the school the ethos and background of their area. They will reflect the experience of its streets and houses, the facilities and atmosphere of the area. They are mirrors of its affluence or poverty, its hope or its frustrations.

The village school served such a clearly defined population, identifiable within the Parish boundary. But that Community, with its population living and working in close proximity to a centre, is a far cry from the urban population and the schools that attempt to meet the educational needs of children from the city environment.

And what of that other aspect of community, the Community of Interest, recognisable to the outsider, valuable and essential to the insider? How does that come across within the school? In the case of Voluntary Aided schools, it is this very Community of Interest that is the determining reason for the existence of the school. Its geographical placement is to a degree incidental; it exists to serve the Community that demanded the school be built. Because of this, such schools develop a particular ethos of their own and we would expect to find within such a school recognisable features that reflect that source Community. Such schools are usually founded out of religious belief, with the clear and express intention of assisting the youth of that religious community to grow up within the tenets, beliefs and practices held by that Community. It is not without significance that the first instruction given to the clergy of the Roman Catholic Community of England and Wales following the restoration of the Hierarchy in 1851, was to found a Parish School.

(ii) Where does that community come from and go to?

The answers that might be offered to that question are indeed numerous and can only be answered in reference to a particular school. But it is a question that must be asked if we are to understand what is going to happen within the confines of the school. Without a sensitive appreciation of the circumstances beyond the school gate our approach to pupils may give rise to misunderstanding and confusion.

When asking where the community comes from we are not just interested in the house number and the street, although this can be significant in itself. We are asking much more than this. We are recognising that the network of relationships within the family units, the transitory nature of some families domicile within the area, the work opportunities, the social opportunities, the social facilities, all affect the child and are reflected in the story that each child brings with them.

Where they go to might be seen, for example, in the restricted sense of school transfer from Primary to Secondary. For the pupils concerned, and their families, this can be of crucial importance. But where do they go to each evening, what do they take back into the community from the school experience? In fact, just how influential is the school on that Community? Does it operate as an agent for effective change? And where are the checks and balances that will govern and regulate such school-centred change? Should not the school respond to needs of the Community it serves? The issues raised by these questions are the subject of considerable discussion elsewhere and it is not necessary that we persue them here. But our response to such questions can greatly determine our approach to the pattern of Assembly within our schools in the light of the 88 Act.

(iii) Multicultural/Multifaith background?

The last thirty years have seen a significant change in the cultural background and religious adherence of large sections of population within our cities. Our schools have had to come to terms with a whole range of circumstances that were not within our experience at the time of the framing of the 44 Act. The effect of this societal change is not to be felt exclusively within those schools serving areas that have experienced such change in its most radical form. If we are to be really serious about the development of an integrated multicultural society, then the entire educational network should be open to the consequence of changed circumstances.

A vital aspect of such a multicultural society must be the acceptance that we now live in a multifaith society, that alongside the Christian Faith which is the heritage of Western Europe, other beliefs and practices are sincerely held and followed and are therefore of real significance to the people from those particular

Communities of Interest. And maybe of even greater significance is the 'society of non-belief', not necessarily of active hostility to religious faith and practice, but the non-belief that comes from indifference. With such indifference comes inexperience and ignorance. The very word 'faith' is a word apart. It is this problem that we must now turn to in our consideration of the Assembly as Worship.

(3)
The Assembly as Worship

(i) The necessary experience of Worship

Each day we should start with an Act of Worship involving the whole school community. What in this sense is meant by an 'Act' and how are we to define 'Worship'?

We have already hinted that our School Community is subject to many influences, some of which will support the creation of a more or less homogenous school society. But we cannot depend on this. It is no use expecting something that isn't there. We have to work from the situation as we find it.

If this Community is to experience together an *Act* of Worship this would suggest that they have some experience of a liturgy outside of the school, something to draw upon, some ground of expressing a personal faith. And if this particular action is to be one of *Worship* then it is suggesting that there must be a goal towards which this faith is directed. We presume on this background of experience, of a life of faith, that is in fact all too often absent. In such circumstances, where does that place our Assembly as an *Act of Worship*? Is it the role of the school in such circumstances to fill the void, to attempt to offer what is essentially a new experience, to develop a liturgy that is indeed meaningful to the pupils and to direct this liturgy towards a definite purpose – God? The 88 Act would suggest that this is so.

(ii) Worship for a defined community of interest

For those schools that have grown out of, or presently serve, a particular Community, the Voluntary Aided Schools, where there is a shared public Liturgy, accepted in practice and directed in purpose, the issue is less confused. They know where the starting points are to be found, they can pick up the threads of that common ground and develop their own liturgy of Worship that is not in conflict with the source community. More than this, they can positively contribute to the growth of a meaningful celebration of belief within that community by offering an understanding of the needs of the young person within that essentially adult orientated world. The community of Interest is strong and purposeful. It should be the ideal situation for real cooperation between home community and school community.

The changing circumstances that voluntary aided schools must now face arises from admission of pupils from beyond the immediate confines of the original social/religious grouping served by the school. If such schools are to continue to offer a particular home of belief then they must recognise that the common identity of pupils can no longer be taken for granted. They too must operate within a pluralistic society and come to terms with the consequences of a new admissions policy.

(iii) Integrity of Worship

Integrity of Worship is concerned with the essential honesty of what we are doing. An Act of Worship implies participation with clear intent. A worshipping community should not be one that is engaging in play acting, albeit for good intentions. Either our Assemblies are Acts of Worship or they are not. If they are not, then we can surely put together a valuable and thoughtful presentation, but don't let us use a term such as Act of Worship, for that it is not.

Young people are very good at seeing through the actions and intentions of adults. They can spot the phony very easily and are not slow to react to what they regard as dishonesty. In the end we do a great dis-service to the possibility of their acquiring 'faith' (if that is indeed an element of our shared Worship). The prayer that is said without understanding or intention might give utterance to familiar words, it might give the impression of Worship to the adults, but what sort of messages is it giving to the children? Equally, our integrity of Worship must recognise the conscience of the pupils (and of staff) with whom we are attempting to pray. Within the detail of the 88 Act parents can withdraw children on conscience grounds and teachers may indicate to the Headteacher their unwillingness to attend.

(4)
The element of participation

(i) Who presides?

Presidency or simply leadership at any gathering that has a degree of formality about it, is important. Who 'presides' sends certain signals to the group, it says something about the nature of the gathering, points up the relationships that are openly acknowledged or implicitly held. Not only is the *person* of this leadership significant but the manner in which the function is fulfilled suggests the degree of importance attached to the occasion by the president.

Such a word might seem rather grand for the occasion of a School Assembly. If the occasion is one of some importance within the corporate life of the school, then the tone and attitude set by the person who is the instigator and enabler is important enough to warrant the use of the term.

If it is an Assembly of the whole school it is likely that the Headteacher or a Deputy will preside. But in many other situations where smaller units are Assembling, it may be Year Coordinator, a House leader or other staff member who takes this role.

It may even be on some occasions that this duty is given to a pupil. Unlikely in the case of younger pupils in the Primary School but a very real possibility in the case of Sixth Form students in Secondary school.

Whoever undertakes the role, it is a crucial one, setting as it does the whole tone and manner of what takes place. It demands preparation and thought if it is to be effectively carried out. Obviously, with experience, the amount of preparation required will vary. But even years of such experience is no substitute for careful thought beforehand, making the most of a particular situation.

(ii) Interactive Assembly – a shared experience.

It was mentioned earlier that on many occasions staff talk at children. There must be an element of participation if the Assembly is to effectively involve the gathered community. The degree will vary with circumstances, but there should be something of a participatory nature about every Assembly.

The attention of the group has to be held, their assent to the experience obtained. Otherwise, what is the point of the exercise? If some are bored, another group distracted, and further sections not understanding a word that is being said, then an extended break might have been more beneficial and certainly less effort.

This is not to say that we shouldn't expect children to listen with attention and be willing to bring the necessary effort to such an occasion, for that in itself is an essential aspect of interaction. But equally we should also look for opportunities when it is possible to seek a positive contribution from the group who have apparently come to hear, making them in a real sense part of the design.

It should be an event that is looked forward to with a degree of anticipation, not seen as a formality that fills a particular slot at the start of the day. If such an ideal is to be achieved then it will not be without effort, care and preparation.

(iii) The shared experience of Prayer

The presentation aspect of the Assembly is straight forward in that the elements used in its construction can be taken directly from the world of experience of pupils. But what of the element of prayer, which if we are to talk of our Assembly as an Act of Worship, must have some place?

It does of course very much depend on our interpretation of 'prayer', how such prayer is made apparent and the degree of active response expected by the children. As was mentioned earlier, the pattern that Prayer will take in an Assembly will be influenced by the nature of the Community which goes to form the school. But it is a two-way process, for the Communal Prayer of Assembly should in the end have a seminal effect on the nature of the school life. This particular problem is picked up again in the final section under the general heading of 'Prayers at Assembly'.

It is the *experience* of prayer that is important, for rather like riding a bike, it is the practical experience of prayer that leads to a deeper understanding of Man's need to pray. Our halting efforts and the real example of others (not the pretend utterance of the right sort of words at the appropriate time) may lead towards some understanding that an Assembly as an Act of Worship has some purpose.

(5)
The need for preparation

(i) Over a period of days where possible – a Curricula approach

It stands to reason that something well prepared is more likely to be effective than something that is rushed and hastily put together. The preparation in no way diminishes the sincerity of the action, rather it enhances it. Our concern to 'get it right' means that the actions we are considering are of some importance. This concern will be transmitted to the pupils and they too will begin to take the view that this is something worth taking time and care over.

The theme of an Assembly might arise in a number of ways and in the next section we will be paying particular concern to content. Two main avenues of approach might be identified here. The first is the selection of a theme for no other reason than it interests the group involved. It might be topical by way of being newsworthy or it might reflect some aspect of religious celebration pertinent to the time and place.

The second might be termed the curricula approach, where the Assembly is the outcome and in some way the culmination of designed classroom experience. It becomes the presentation of the learning activity to others, it is truly a sharing of work, a remaking of acquired skills and knowledge for others, a celebration of the classroom.

Such an approach allows for the Assembly to be the natural outcome of planned teaching rather than imposing an artificial 'let's do an Assembly' attitude. It signals to the children that the work being undertaken has value not only to them but to a greater audience. The secular work of the classroom is given a greater significance for being included in an occasion where the Community celebrates, where the Community in fact, Worships.

This period of preparation might be weeks, it might be days. But from the outset it must be clear to the group that the end product of their cooperative working will be the Assembly, maybe on one or more occasions.

Even if a specific topic is selected that is not a part of the long term planned curricula at a particular time, then this too can be worked up over a period of days, the necessary reading, acting and painting being made part of classroom activity.

For this reason, it is very useful to publish, a term in advance, just who will be responsible for which Assembly. In this way due consideration of themes can be given in the planning of units of work. But even such foresight cannot take in to account that some Assemblies will just not fit that model of development.

(ii) The survivalist approach

There are some occasions (one might even say, many occasions) when it is just not possible to plan ahead in the way described above. This is particularly true in the case of the Headteacher who regularly has to take an Assembly.

To begin with, it is quite likely that the Head does not have a class group that can be directed over a period of days towards a clearly defined goal. It might be possible to have some discussion with a group of children the day before the Assembly is due to take place. If readings of any complexity are to be used, then this is almost essential, unless the pupils taking part have reading skills that can cope with a text offered at very short notice.

The texts of the Assemblies offered as examples in the second half of this book are reworded from original texts used at Assemblies, often written at very short notice and presented without lengthy preparation. The particular theme may well have been given some consideration earlier, particularly if music was required. It was however possible to produce Assemblies that were relevant, interesting, informative and to varying degrees worshipful.

Maybe not an approach to be recommended, but one that can work if there is an understanding of the Assembly within the context of the community sharing the experience. After a while, you know what will 'work' and what won't. The danger is that a pattern is established that might become tedious if variations aren't actively sought.

(iii) The care with texts

Anything that we ask a child to read should be intelligible to the reader first and through the reader's understanding, meaningful to the listener. This will only be achieved if we show great care with the texts that we ask children to use.

Care first in what we might write for them and ask them to read. Secondly care in the choice of published texts that we offer them, be it an excerpt from an appropriate novel, a poem or a passage from Scripture. The words must have meaning that is accessible. Otherwise, we have children listening to sounds that offer spaces between activity.

Texts therefore that are appropriate to the age of the reader must be an essential prerequisite for use in an Assembly. Most appropriate of all is the written work of children, read aloud by themselves or by others.

(6)
The immediacy of content

(i) The assembly as an expression of current news

An Assembly is essentially topical. It is a gathering of the School Community at a particular moment in time, an occasion when they expect to hear the latest news of events that directly affect themselves.

Why not therefore pick up events from beyond the confines of the school environment and use these as the foundation of an Assembly theme? It is an opportunity to explain, to relate in suitable language, material being treated by the media, a chance to draw suitable stories from the real world rather than rely on the story or fable from the historical past which might or might not have relevance.

A note of caution must be raised. We are all too aware that on a number of occasions the media treatment, particularly of disaster situations, can be excessively intrusive, apparently intent on the hype of a news event only to satisfy the inquisitive public. If such a story is picked up for an Assembly Theme it should be handled with sensitivity and care. We are responsible to a captive audience who cannot change channels or walk out if they don't like what they hear.

(ii) The relating of the Scriptures to real, known events.

Just as we have picked up items of news or particular events and suggested that they might fruitfully be used as themes, so too opportunity can occur for the relating of the Scriptures to such current affairs. What, after all, were the parables of the New Testament? Nothing other than the telling of a story about a real situation, familiar to the listeners, and then drawing from it a moral, philosophical or theological meaning. They were a means of communicating in a manner that was easily comprehendible to the people of the time.

Our Assembly is not that far removed from such circumstances. We are in the communication business and should therefore look to the various approaches that are possible to meet the needs of the listeners. Themes of care, of concern, of choice, of action in difficult circumstances, of heroism in the face of danger, of moral decision where particular actions affect our own lives or the lives of others, all have a reflection within the Scriptural background of the Old and New Testaments. And what of the writings and foundation texts of other Faiths? Maybe we can fruitfully explore a literature that is unfamiliar to us and therefore ignored and neglected. There is an evident need for an introduction to and summary of such textual material for teachers whose own background is within the Western (and therefore historically Christian) tradition. Although they may not themselves be adherents to a Christian Faith they are never the less aware of the literary tradition that exists within the Christian cultural background.

(iii) The use of child-centred events

In our enthusiasm to look outside of the school, bringing local or national events into our Assembly, don't let us forget the most important source that we have is within the school, the pupils themselves. They have stories that should be told, either as the direct result of events that have occurred in the school environment or in their experience out of school.

Possibly there are greater opportunities in the Primary school to tap such a source, where children are more likely, to share the day to day 'out of school' experiences with their teachers. At Secondary level, we might have to dig a little deeper to reach the detail that is there. Encouraging pupils in their teens to talk about such events is not always easy. But if it can be achieved, the result is well worth the effort.

(7)
The circumstances of the Assembly

(i) The layout of the Hall: First Impressions

The setting in which particular events take place contributes to their success. We enjoy the detail of the event, but part of that enjoyment is the experience of the circumstances and location in which such an occasion is located. And first impressions count. They can set the tone of excitement, of anticipation, or the very opposite of expectant boredom and switch-off.

We must pay some attention therefore to the Hall or other space that is to be used for Assembly. We must use it creatively, looking carefully at the opportunities it offers as an area for activity. Where, for example, is the focus of that Assembly's action to be located? Will pupils (and staff) on arrival be given any indication of what is to happen on that occasion? Will they, in fact, be welcomed? And what about the lighting of the room? Great changes in mood can be set by imaginative use of lights, curtains, free standing lamps, or even with care, candles.

Who will sit where? Will pupils sit on chairs or on the floor? Where will the staff sit? Who will greet them? What will be the signals that tell people present that we are ready to start? These questions should be considered by the staff if some framework that is understood by all is to be agreed.

There is a degree of formality to such an occasion. Yet that formality should be implied, a hidden understructure rather than an obtrusive pattern of behaviour. Tone is important. It helps to create an atmosphere where both adults and children are receptive and open to events that they are about to experience.

(ii) Presentation: Arrival and Departure

The actual arrival of pupils and staff is in fact the start of the Assembly, even though the designed events of that morning have not yet formally begun. The way in which groups arrive can ensure the right atmosphere or otherwise. They should know where to go if there is a 'usual' pattern of places or have any alterations clearly indicated to them.

If music is part of their arrival, then the choice of that music should if possible reflect something of the theme of the Assembly. Music played just for the sake of a sound adds little to the start of an Assembly, but just becomes background noise of little consequence. There may well be an occasion when the most effective background to the arrival of pupils is silence.

Just as the settling of the group at the start of the Assembly determines a good start, so the manner in which the pupils leave at the end of the Assembly is also important. If the Assembly has indeed been thought provoking, then the leaving procedures should allow for a reflection of events just experienced.

Whatever has been the content of the Assembly, whatever notices or comments have been made at the end, however much the mood might have changed during the preceding quarter of an hour, bring back the theme at the dismissal time, either by a comment or by music. In this way, the focus of attention is brought back to the president of the Assembly, and the story that has been told is drawn to a conclusion. It may also be the opportunity to point towards the next occasion of meeting.

Either way, pupils can leave the hall in a sensible and orderly manner, preferably with indication for a group at a time to move.

(iii) The role of the staff

The staff will have been responsible for bringing the pupils to the Assembly. It is too easy for them to assume then that their role is over, that the president of the Assembly takes charge and is responsible for all that follows. For the staff to sit down and take no further part (or worse still to use the Assembly as an occasion to catch up on gossip) is to deny the very communal sharing that is the responsibility and opportunity of all participants.

Equally, in exercising control over groups of children, an excessive use of a raised voice adds little to the attempt to create a reflective and attentive atmosphere. As much, if not more, can be achieved by indications with hand or eye and physical presence, as by the voice. The willingness of the staff to be part of the occasion will transmit itself to the children just as clearly as their disinterested behaviour will be taken as an example to follow.

At the end of the Assembly, as groups are sent out of the hall, it is equally the responsibility of staff to take back into their charge pupils assigned to them, allowing the main participants in the Assembly a low key role after the events of the morning in which they have been the principal players.

Depending on the nature of the activity that immediately follows such an Assembly, it can be very valuable and informative for staff to discuss with their groups the details of the presentation. This can be seen as another aspect of the 'interactive Assembly', only that the interaction is not taking place in the Assembly room. Besides, some discussion is much better undertaken in small groups than attempting analysis with many present. It may well help to point out the direction of action that might arise out of the Assembly. Where there has been an issue that may be controversial or emotionally challenging to the pupils, then such a 'debriefing' is almost essential as part of the total experience of the Assembly.

(8)
The Assembly presented to the wider community

(i) When shall we invite the Parents?

There is a clear purpose and need for Assembly that is a celebration within the School Community. Such an action is seen as part of the daily life of the school. But there are other occasions when it is good to open the doors and invite others to share in that experience. The parents of the pupils are the most obvious audience that we should consider. And maybe 'audience' is the wrong word within the context of an 'inter-active'; 'invited participants' might be better. Just how we involve them and to what degree, will depend very much on the Theme of the Assembly. It might be that they can bring something into the Assembly to show the children, or talk to them about some local event, or take part by reading a prepared passage. Remember, just as children need time to come to terms with standing up in front of their peer group, so too do parents. They are not necessarily used to public presentation and haven't the professional skills that teachers acquire. Don't offer them a text the moment they arrive at the school and so put them off ever venturing in again in case they get landed with something to do.

Make the invitation to parents part of the Assembly preparation. The letter home, particularly when written by younger children, is much harder to ignore than the casual throw-away remark over tea (or even breakfast) that 'You can come to school if you want, I'm reading.'

The invitation to Assembly is an excellent way of making contact with parents on an occasion that is a non-threatening relationship between home and school. No-one is in trouble, they are not coming to school because of a particular problem. They come as welcome members of the larger Community that the school serves. They come to participate in the activity of their children, to celebrate with them, to share in the action of Worship.

We should make them feel welcome from the moment they arrive. We should arrange for children to greet them and show them to their places. We should put them at their ease so that they become an accepted part of the scene and not a line of adults sat on show, feeling awkward and embarrassed.

At the end of the Assembly, someone should thank them for coming, not necessarily the president of the Assembly, and if the circumstances make it possible, they should be invited to stay for a cup of tea or coffee – the charge for which should be a justifiable expense against School Funds. In this way, people will not come to feel that every time they go to school they have to open their purse.

This is the opportunity for meeting parents in an informal manner, getting to know them and allowing them to get to know staff of the school other than across the table on Parents' Evening or through the doubtful hearsay of their children.

It can also be the setting for discussion about the Assembly in the same way as has been suggested between staff and pupils

(ii) Are there other local groups who could share our Assembly?

The invitation to parents and to their friends and relations should not be the limit of our contact with the 'world outside'. The very theme of the Assembly might determine who comes and what they do when they arrive.

It might be that they are involved in some particular enterprise that is currently important to the school and their presence adds to the interest of the Assembly. They may well be asked to make a contribution, again with prior knowledge to allow for preparation.

They might be the subject of a presentation from the school, possibly at the time of a Harvest Festival or following a community involvement project.

It might even be another school. We meet each other on the sports field, why not now and then in the different setting of the School Assembly?

Who does in fact come will depend on the situation of the school and it should be part of the Assembly preparation to seek out the possibilities of invited guests.

(ii) And who shall we invite this time? – and what is the intention of the invite?

There are some guests we might consider inviting for totally different reasons. They may well have some formal relationship with the school community and so will be welcomed on a different footing to other guests already mentioned.

For example, the School Governors should be invited to share Assembly from time to time. They have a responsible function to exercise as Governors under the 88 Act. It is only right therefore that opportunity should be afforded to them to see something of the Community in its daily life. If they do come, make them welcome and above all, let the children know who they are and why they are in school. Otherwise something is lost from their visit.

The local clergy, or other Community leaders, should also be made to feel welcome and encouraged to come along. There will be a number of occasions when they will be able to play an active role in the detail of the assembly. But their invitation should not be restricted to Assemblies where such participation is expected.

Look around the local community and see who else might be invited. Local councillors, local industry and business management as well as professional colleagues either from other schools or from the Inspectorate. All can be made welcome.

It does work both ways, for there may well be an occasion when as a school we need their support. Much easier to ask for it if there has already been occasion for some shared understanding of the daily life of the school.

(9)
The resources for an Assembly

(i) Pictures, posters, the art work of the school

Mention was made earlier of the need for the place of Assembly to be welcoming. Part of such a welcome is the display that might accompany the presentation. The brightness and interest of material brought to the Assembly can not only enhance the actual event. It can also serve to extend the experience in the days that follow by being an ever-present reminder to passing groups of what has taken place.

If the Assembly area also has other functions (such as the hall for PE, a dining area or a teaching area for music) then it may well be impossible to leave much material on free standing display. It is for this reason that good display boards should be available that will allow for material to remain behind after the Assembly has finished. These can either be permanent fixtures to the wall or movable units which can be relocated as the use of the hall changes through the day. In neither case need such display areas be that extensive. Bearing in mind that during the actual Assembly there will not be a great deal of time to closely observe such material, a smaller number of carefully chosen items can in the end serve to create a greater impact.

Such material might be commercially produced posters and pictures, whose size and quality make them ideal material for such display. Equally, the art work produced by children in association with the Assembly theme should be used. In the Primary sector where it is easier through an integrated approach to develop such material, this option is more readily attractive. With some pre-planning it can be arranged with older pupils as well.

But whatever the source, the inclusion of visually stimulating material, be it pictorial or objective in form, adds to the scene. It makes the occasion different, in some way it enhances words and actions. It makes the content memorable, it is a fragment towards the completion of the whole and without it there would be something of quality lost.

(ii) Simple clothing props – a minimal list of useful items.

The Assembly is not the occasion for a full blown dramatic production. However, the use of a few items of clothing can greatly assist the telling of a story. Ideally they should be kept near to the Assembly area, so that if they are required in a hurry they are readily accessible.

What to include? Obviously the list could be endless, but given the finite storage facility that is available, how might such a list be reduced to its essentials? The following items might be considered worthwhile including:

> a couple of hats, some large shawls, an overcoat, a dress, a jacket, a skirt, a pair of trousers, a pair of gloves, a pair of glasses, a wig or two...

It can be added to as materials become available and should in any case be changed every so often. The same hat and coat appearing week after week does tend to reduce the interest value of the items.

(iii) The odd block, table and occasional chair.

The need for other items will constantly change and they can be brought to the hall as required. It is useful though to know what is readily available within the hall, props that can be brought into use very quickly and easily.

One or two rostra blocks of different heights to help give varying levels to actions or to readings are valuable. Make sure that endless use does not reduce them to a state of distracting tattiness. The occasional coat of paint, or at least the covering of the sides with sugar paper, does help. A piece of carpet tacked to the top also reduces the noise level when movement takes place.

A table, maybe a low coffee table, can be most useful. That and an easy chair give the president of the Assembly somewhere to sit, and so provide a focal point round which the action of the Assembly can centre. It is a place to put things, papers, certificates, hymn books etc. when not in use.

And finally, how about a large bean bag or two and some small carpet offcuts? Chairs are not always the most appropriate location for pupils presenting the Assembly. They can make for a formality that is an interference in the action of the Assembly. What can be kept will depend on the storage area that is available.

(10)
The purposeful use of Music

(i) Tapes and records: chosen with design.
An integral part of the assembly.

Music is a very important element within the planning and presentation of an Assembly. The choice of music requires thoughtful selection for it is not to be seen as an extra, tagged on as an after thought. It should be incorporated because it has value, because it adds to the experience of the story and should therefore be included at an early stage of preparation.

What sort of music should we consider? Anything that serves our purpose must be the answer. There is a richness in the lyrics and music of the last twenty years that shouldn't be ignored. The words of many of these songs can be incorporated into the Assembly adding a new dimension to the spoken words of pupils and staff.

It should be relevant to the experience of the children without pandering to the passing tastes and nine day wonders of the pop chart. Pick and choose with a bit of thought. Try to build up a stock of useful tapes and records within the school of performers whose material may be useful. Above all, be open to suggestions from others who may know of music that is unfamiliar, but still worth a listen.

Apart from the world of popular music, folk music or indeed classical sources, there are a number of compilations now available of music and songs specifically for Worship or Meditation. Collections of modern hymns, recordings by church groups or tapes from inter denominational groups such as the community of Taizé in France. This is new music, music of our time. It is relevant to our purpose, it is there to be used, there to be learnt.

It might have started its life in the secular field but that is no reason why a good lyric should not be put to good purpose elsewhere. Too easily we create a divide between what is secular and what is not. It is the very unity of the experience of life that we should be offering our pupils. Maybe that interpretation of the words *Act of Worship* would allow us to move on beyond what appears to be a constriction on our action. It is certainly worth considering.

(ii) Live music provided by the children

Nothing substitutes for live music, the creation of those taking part, the results of their own endeavours.

It might be that a group who have been under instruction from peripatetic staff will wish to use the forum of the Assembly as the occasion for displaying their maturing skills. The music they offer does not necessarily have to fit in some obtruse way with a particular theme. Lets enjoy the celebration of their playing.

There may be opportunity for pupils to accompany the school in the singing of a hymn using a variety of instruments. Fine, if it is possible. Or it may just be that a single accompaniment to a reading is all that is called for. Whilst always seeking after excellence, we should not be put off accepting the offer to participate even if the result is not the perfection we might have liked. It is what the child can bring that is important, it is their contribution that we accept.

Nor should the staff contribution be limited to the piano accompaniment for hymns. Ask around, it is quite surprising who can play some other instrument and who with some careful persuasion might add a new colour to the Assembly.

(iii) The choice of hymns

Hymns live within particular traditions and come to have associations for the singers which gives them value over and above (and one might be tempted to say, inspite of) the words of the text.

People recognise some songs as hymns, they have that 'churchy' sound and the tunes seem bound in a time that has long since passed. For many of the children they will have no other experience of hymns, they will have no real understanding of their history or of their use. So the choice of a hymn has to be something that recognises this background. Better to have nothing at all than a hymn stuck on the end without rhyme or reason, whose language carries no meaning for the singers, pupils and adults alike.

It is sometimes of interest to read the words first as part of the Assembly, give time and consideration to their form and meaning so that the singing of them does have a purpose. This should certainly be an element of hymn practice, for how can one sing well when really there is no comprehension of the text?

The purchase of many copies of just one hymn book can be restrictive. Better to choose four books and buy in smaller quantities. There is no reason why everyone should have a book, why a small group might not sing the hymn or prayer on behalf of everyone. The others will soon learn the words and tune in any case.

(11)
The need to be heard

(i) Simple amplification – education in the use of the microphone

The time taken in the preparation of an Assembly is often wasted when children cannot be heard by the assembled group. Some children have naturally quiet voices, others are shy, others hesitant. Why not help them (and their listeners) by using microphones?

This does not in any way diminish the need to develop confidence in children and use of their own voice, and that we will come to shortly. But at this point let's consider the advantages that arise from the use of microphones.

In the preparation of the text, emphasis can be placed on the meaning and presentation of that text without worry about the size of the room or the degree of confidence that the reader might have. It is too easy to ask the same small group of children to read because we are confident in their ability to handle a text in a manner which will ensure quality in 'performance'. As a result many children who may well like to read are left on the sidelines.

Careful and intelligent use of amplification can help to overcome this problem and open to a much wider group the possibility of making a valued contribution to the Assembly. The view often expressed that a microphone limits the development of speaking skills is not born out in practice. The quality of sound and the attention of the group are in the end far more supportive to the child, encouraging participation.

A good microphone stand and a good quality microphone are essential. Otherwise the tone of voice can be distorted and the consequent result a distraction rather than an improvement. Children need to be shown how to adjust the height of the microphone as well as its angle. With some systems it is possible to 'voice over' music and the resultant background of music to the voice can produce some interesting effects.

(ii) Presentation of voice and presence of person

The public presentation of language is very different from the conversational language that is the currency of every day communication for children. They have to be shown how to present themselves, how to gain the attention of listeners before they speak and how to use their voice to maintain that interest.

The natural nervousness that some children experience when asked to read can result in a rushed reading, head lowered with the final few words being spoken as they turn and hurry back to their place. Coming to a microphone to read has the added value that it is an immediate point of location for the reader, the necessary adjustment to the stand giving them a few seconds pause before they turn to their script. They must then be encouraged to stay right to the end of text, for any turning away from the microphone is immediately noticeable. The use of amplification thus helps to highlight this problem, making children aware of the consequences of their early movement. Their 'presence' is important.

(iii) Confidence grows through experiences

Throughout this discussion of the Assembly, we have spoken of the Assembly itself, its theme and the Community sharing the experience. Maybe this is the appropriate time to turn the issue the other way and ask questions about the participants – what of their experience?

Quite apart from any need to meet the requirements of the Act of Worship, or the Community need of gathering together, the presentation of an Assembly has some very positive educational value to those who prepare it. Provided that we do not take the elitist view that only the quality of the end product matters, then the participation of all pupils gives them a chance to develop self-confidence.

It also signals to the whole of the school community that each person has value, that each has a contribution to make.

(12)
The dramatic presentation

(i) Simple use of scripts

The Assemblies offered later in this book have all been developed round the use of simple scripts, not in the sense of 'part reading' but as a narrative thread running through the Assembly, linked by either music or some simple dramatic presentation.

Such scripts can take two main forms. They can be the writing of pupils based on a specific thematic development or can be written by one person enabling some cohesion to be given to the text. It was in the latter form that these Assemblies arose.

A few obvious points. The script should be clearly written, typed if possible, for it is often taxing enough for the reader to handle the reading in public, without the added problem of struggling to interpret poorly written or badly reproduced material. Indications can be noted on the script for pauses, emphasis, music etc.

As part of the concern for presentation, back the sheets with card or stiff paper. It makes the handling of the page much easier and in any case looks better.

If microphones are being used, the reader needs to be shown where to hold the script so that it doesn't get in the way of the microphone head or continually knock against the stand so creating noise disturbance. On some occasions a lectern might be used. Make certain that it fulfils the purpose of a place for texts rather than an unfortunate hiding place for a small child peering anxiously over its edge.

(ii) The preparation of the 'small' event

For some, the term 'drama' implies productions, lights, makeup and costume. This is not necessary nor indeed is it appropriate to most Assembly situations. This should not, however, preclude the use of dramatic presentation, the 'small event' that serves to highlight a reading, that helps develop a story, that explains and supports a particular text. Such scenes will almost always be improvised, the basic idea being discussed with a group of children who are then able to present their own perspective of the event.

The lighting, the props, the costume will be minimal. It will not be lengthy, often only a few minutes, but it should be to the point, clear in intention, supportive of the central theme. The attempt at longevity usually result in the loss of attention by the group watching and so the whole purpose of the introduction of drama is lost and the Assembly is flawed as an event of celebration.

(iii) Drama for meaning – not to outdo last week's offering

The Assembly is not the occasion for competition, but it is the time when careful consideration and preparation should result in something that is sincere and honest.

The need to vary approaches can lead to apparent competition. But this variety is essential and the lack of it is one of the major stumbling blocks that face those responsible for the structure and format of the Assembly.

If the whole thing is predictable, if the pattern never changes, then the real opportunities that the occasion offers are lost and pupils come in not expecting any particular lift and come away with their expectations duly satisfied.

In looking for such variety, we mustn't lose sight of our purpose, but don't let it become a straight jacket that precludes a divergent approach to the problem.

(13)
Texts for Assemblies

(i) Scripture that children can understand

When asking children to read from scripture, give some thought to the particular version that you are asking them to use. Texts that are familiar to adults are not necessarily the most suitable for use with younger people.

One of Sydney Carter's songs has the line 'Give me the Good News in the present tense'. There is enough difficulty in the content and historical circumstances of the Old and New Testaments without adding linguistic difficulties of archaic English.

It can also help considerably to the understanding of a reading if there are a few words of introduction. Some comment on where the reading has come from, who wrote it and when, the historical/geographical circumstances that were the setting for the writing, all help to place the reading within some framework. Otherwise the reading is rootless, it has come from nowhere, is unrelated to anything in particular and will accordingly be soon forgotten.

The Assembly may be considered as a starting point from which further discovery might later be made. Such detail is valuable. It need not take long.

(ii) Secular readings of suitable content

Scriptural sources are by no means the only sorce of suitable material for use at an Assembly. If we start from the standpoint that anything might indeed be suitable, then we open for use the whole range of literature. The selection from that vast range of available material will depend on the particular theme of the Assembly and the age of the pupils involved. Don't select material that is beyond the understanding of the children, but at the same time don't be afraid of presenting them with something that might offer some challenge both in content and style.

As in the instance of readings from Scripture, place the reading in some context, where it is from, who wrote it and a brief comment on events described just prior to the extract that is about to be read.

(iii) Children's own writing

We have already mentioned the value of using children's own writing in the Assembly, for just as the experience of reading aloud or taking part in some simple dramatic presentation can be of great value in their own personal development, the same holds true for the written word.

Too often, the writing that we ask children to undertake doesn't, from the child's viewpoint, have real purpose. In the case of something written for use in the Assembly, we are not only asking for the writing to be done, we are making clear the purpose to which the end result will be put.

It is not always necessary that the writer should read their own work; in fact there are some occasions when there is positive merit in another voice other than the writer's being heard. However, remember again to acknowledge the writer. It is their work, their contribution, they deserve to be recognised.

It might be that the piece of writing is produced specifically for that Assembly. On the other hand there is no reason not to include work which has arisen directly from other classroom activity.

(14)
Prayers at Assembly

(i) Well-known prayers of the Christian tradition.

We come to perhaps the hardest element of all in the design of the Assembly, for when we consider Prayer we are face to face with the problems associated with 'Worship' and with 'Community' and the need to respect the position of the individual.

In casting round for suitable prayers that might be used, we should therefore bear in mind not only the differing strands of Christian practice but also that some pupils may be sincere participants of a non-Christian faith, or come from a background that is in the true sense of the word Pagan, lacking any allegiance, devoid of any concern for, or need of, prayer.

What do we do? First we must offer variety, a selection of prayers that offer the children the experience of differing textual approaches. Secondly, we must try to talk to them about Prayer, its form, its purpose. Unless someone is willing to share with them such personal experience, they have little chance of understanding the mysterious, yet vital, place that Prayer has in the lives of countless millions of people throughout the world.

They need to be introduced to the tradition of prayer, to its changing language in time, to understand that each generation tries to find its own way of expressing deep and fundamental thoughts and feelings about itself and God.

(ii) Contemporary prayers

Just as the hymns of the last century might have fulfilled a need within the language and sentiment of that time, so the prayers of earlier Christian communities may not ring with the same truth to the current generation. This is not to say that we should reject material which by nature of its age is no longer contemporary. Part of the heritage that we have to share with children is the transmission of a cultural tradition; religious belief and its expression are part of that tradition and require understanding.

Part of that understanding is the realisation that this process is still continuing. There are still men and women who, looking at the Gospels and the Christian tradition, are representing to modern man the same truths. But the words of that new view are the words of contemporary society.

We too must seek out this new ground, for otherwise we offer our pupils something which is historically stunted. Their whole view of the religious experience, and in consequence the words 'Act of Worship' is framed within a historical pattern that has no relevance to the here and now.

(iii) Prayers written by the children

One way of exploring with children the nature of Prayer is to ask them to write their own prayers. Some direction and discussion is obviously required, for a blank sheet of paper and the instruction 'write a prayer' is usually fruitless.

The starting point will vary depending on their experience out of school. Prayer is an expression of man's condition, an attempt to understand where he is and how it all relates a theistic belief. The written form of that yearning emerges as prayer of concern for his own well-being, prayer of thanks for his own continued safety and only much later prayer that is truly concerned at developing his relationship with, and experience of, God.

In school, we can do but little in this direction, and indeed there are some who would argue that this is not the place for any such attempt, that matters of faith are not for the classroom. They may be right. The 88 Act seems to argue a differing point of view. But we cannot avoid considering the very forces that have shaped the society we at present know, we cannot avoid our heritage. It could equally be argued that the great stress within our society is the result of our detachment from that historical reality.

But as long as we have Assemblies which are associated with the phrase Act of Worship, then let us be honest in our approach, not ignoring the issues that are raised in consequence, but openly admitting our difficulties.

Preface note to the sample Assemblies

The Assemblies that follow offer only a skeleton of words around which the Assembly can be built.

Although each Assembly was written and used in a Middle or Primary School they have been stripped of much that was particular to that school at that time.

If they are to be used elsewhere, then care and consideration must be given to the detail that may need to be added.

Very little indication has been made regarding suitable hymns or music except where there is direct mention made in the text. Each school will have its own personal choice of hymns. Other music used will reflect the interests and tastes of staff and pupils. And rightly so.

The arrangement of the words on the page is important, for if children are being asked to read a text, then the more help that can be given to enable them to bring meaning to the words they read, the better. In writing for young people, it is a point worth remembering.

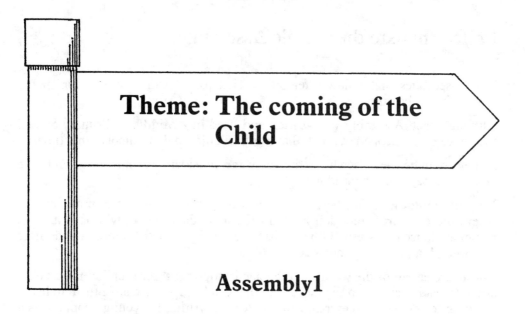

Theme: The coming of the Child

Assembly 1

Reader [1] When we are expecting someone special to pay a visit to our home, we usually tidy up a bit.

Make the place look reasonable, and put away the bits and pieces.

And if it is someone who is very special to us then we will make an extra effort during the days before the visit to get ready.

We will be excited and begin to look forward to the great day of arrival.

Reader [2] If our visitor has to travel a long way to see us, we might well go to the railway station or even the airport.

We would have a meal ready for them at home and we would try to make them as comfortable as we could.

In this way, we could enjoy their visit and they could enjoy being with us.

Reader [3] That is what the Season of Advent is all about:
    a time of getting ready,
    a time of preparation,
    a time of excitement,
    a time of expectation.

But what are we waiting for?

Who is coming?

Reader [4] Are we just waiting for the presents and the parties? For the cards and the pantomimes? Are we just being selfish?

Or will there be some space in our busy days for the story of the Christ Child?

The baby born in the stable, a baby born poor, the Child of Bethlehem.

Reader [5] You see, it is so easy to forget that Christmas is about that Child.

It is about the Good News of His Birth.

> A time of rejoicing,
> a time of happiness,
> a time of hopefulness,
> a time of peace.

Reader [6] Lord,

> Come to us this Christmas
> and bring us,
> each one of us
> the gift of Bethlehem,
> the gift of yourself.
>   Amen

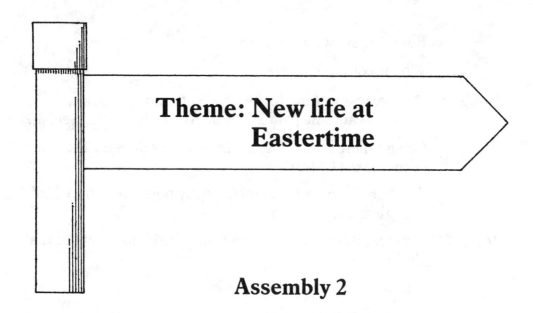

Theme: New life at Eastertime

Assembly 2

Reader [1] It is a damp morning in January, the first month of the year.

> Overnight, it has been cold, with a slight frost in some places.
>
> But now this morning, our star, which we call the Sun, shines through thin cloud, a rich, dark orange colour.
>
> It gives us the light we call day, it warms the earth, helping us to live.

Reader [2] Around us, the trees and plants show little sign of life.

> Many of the trees are bare, their branches reaching out to the sky, stripped of leaves that only a few months ago covered them.
>
> It is hard to believe that from those bare thin twigs will come new leaves, new life in the Spring.

Reader [3] The hedge rows have lost their colour, like the trees. They have sharp twigs pointing to the cold winter sky.

> They too wait for the Spring and the new life that will come.

Reader [4] Some of the birds we see in the warm Summer months have left us and gone south for Winter.

> Only when the weather gets warmer will they return.
>
> Other animals have gone into a long sleep.
>
> In this way they don't use valuable energy.
>
> In the cold weather, they find it very hard to find enough food to keep them alive.

Reader [5] It is very hard when we look about us at this time of the year, to realise that Spring will come.

> Within the ground there is the new life that will come back to our land when the weather is warmer again.
>
> Things that look dark and dead already have the seeds of new life.

Reader [6] This was the hope that the friends of Jesus shared with each other.

> It was the promise that Jesus made to them, of new life with God our Father.
>
> It was the promise of Easter Day, the day He came back to them, after all had seemed lost.
>
> Let us think of that promise as we say together:
>
> "OUR FATHER..."

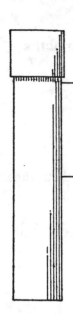

Theme: Silence in a busy world

Assembly 3

Reader [1] SILENCE is the space between words.

> SILENCE is the time of quiet after noise.

Reader [2] SILENCE is the time when we listen.

> SILENCE is the time when we might hear others.

Reader [3] SILENCE is the time of rest after work.

> SILENCE is the time of peace.

Reader [4] We live in a noise-filled world.

> A world of television and radio, of tape recorders and records, videos and computers.

> There is noise in the streets from cars and lorries, buses and motorcycles. The beeping of horns and the screeching of brakes.

> There is noise everywhere.

Reader [5] There is noise in the factories, the noise of machines.

> There is noise in the air, from aircraft.

> No wonder we get tired, no wonder we find it hard to really listen.

> We miss the space between words,
>
> we never hear the silence.
>
> We never notice it, we are so busy.

Reader [6] And so, in our hurry to get on with things, in our excitement, in all our noise, we miss the silence, when for a few moments we might be quiet with God our Father.

> PAUSE

Reader [7] Lord,

> help us,
> > in our own small way,
> > to listen to you.
>
> Lord,
> > Help us,
> > to pause now and then
> > that we might turn to you.
>
> Lord,
> > teach us to understand
> > that unless we listen
> > we will never hear you.

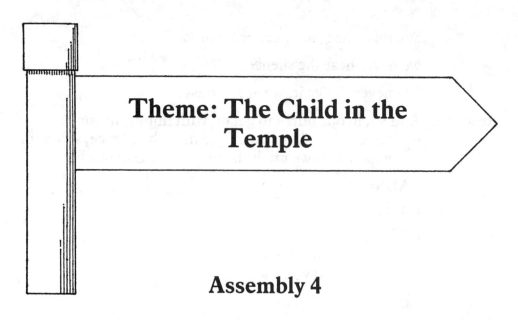

Theme: The Child in the Temple

Assembly 4

Reader [1] When you're grown up, you will understand.

When you're grown up, you will be able to see what I mean,

when you're grown up…

The trouble is, it will be a long time before I'm grown up.

Reader [2] That's the trouble with grown ups, they are always telling us what to do and how to do it and when to do it…

It really does get a bit boring sometimes.

But, the trouble is, they ARE usually right.

Reader [3] We do still have many things to learn, many questions to ask, many mistakes to make.

That is all part of being a child, until when we get older, we become one of the grown ups ourselves.

Reader [4] We would find it very strange, if, one morning when we came to school, we walked into one of our teaching areas and found it full of grown ups with a boy from the top year in charge.

It would seem even sillier, if the grown ups were asking questions and the boy knew all the answers.

The grown ups wouldn't like it, they would really feel put out.

Reader [5] There is just one story in the Gospels that tells us about Jesus as a young boy.

He had been taken by his parents to the city of Jerusalem, for it was a custom of the Hebrew people to bring a boy of twelve to the Temple.

It was the "leaving behind of childhood" time. They left Jerusalem and began the journey home. After a while they realised that Jesus was not with them.

They asked their friends, but he was nowhere to be found.

So they went back and started looking for him. They were worried that he was lost.

Reader [6] When they did find him, he was back in the Temple.

Around him were the grown ups, the priests and the teachers.

They were asking him questions and listening to his answers.

They were very surprised at what they heard.

He seemed to have some very good answers.

Reader [7] Mary, his Mother, wasn't very impressed though, for she had been worried, not knowing where he was.

And she told him so.

Jesus, the young boy of 12, replied:

> Didn't you know,
> I had to attend to my Father's Story?

This term we are looking at rules and their importance — we have looked at what our world would be like without rules and why we should keep them.

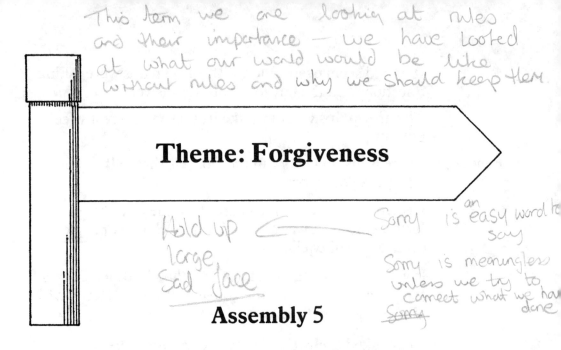

Hold up large, sad face

Sorry is an easy word to say

Sorry is meaningless unless we try to correct what we have done

Theme: Forgiveness

Assembly 5

Reader [1] How many times this week have you made a mistake?

How many times have you done something that has hurt someone else?

And how many times have you been forgiven?

Reader [2] It is a strange word, 'FORGIVEN'.

We often say it:
   'Oh please, forgive me' *(Several children to say what they say it for or who to.)*

but what does it really mean?

children with pictures

We say it when we want to make something good again. When we want to put things right, when we want it to be like it was, before things went wrong.

So we say,
   'Please, forgive me'

Reader [3] It is not a hard word to say:
   FORGIVE
   but sometimes it is a very hard thing to do.

hold up a banner spelling the word

When a great hurt has been done, the forgiveness comes very hard indeed.

It costs a lot, takes a great effort and can be the sign of real love.

Reader [4] Would we believe someone who said

'Oh yes, I forgive you,
but I'm not going to let you forget it'

That wouldn't be much good.

When forgiveness is offered, then a friendship is made good again.

Something that was broken is repaired, something that was causing a problem between people is removed.

A new start can be made.

Reader [5] So it was with Jesus when he spoke to people.

He was always willing to offer them forgiveness. Whatever they had done, he offered them a chance to start again.

A chance to be really forgiven.

Yesterday is gone, we can't do much about it, but today is a new day, a chance to start again.

Reader [6] As we say our prayers together this morning, remember that we can ask God our Father for forgiveness.

But there is a catch.

If we wish to start again, if we want to be forgiven, then we must be willing to forgiven other people.

We must offer the chance of a new start to others if we want one ourselves.

Let us say together:

"OUR FATHER..."

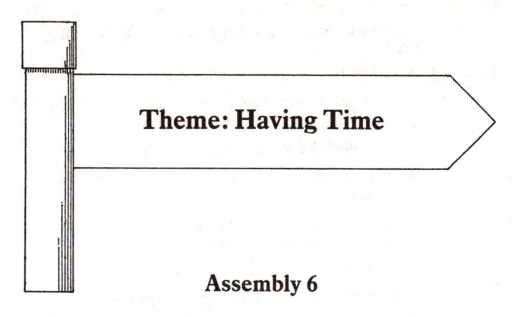

Theme: Having Time

Assembly 6

Reader [1] I'm sorry, but I haven't time. I can't come, I have so much to do. I haven't time.

I would like to help you, but I'm very busy this morning, I haven't got the time. Someone else will have to do it. I haven't time…

How many times have you heard someone say that? I am sorry, but I haven't time.

Reader [2] Time never stops, it never stands still and waits for us. Already you are older now than when you woke up this morning. Each day you grow older and change ever so slightly.

For some of you, that means you are growing taller and heavier, you are changing from children and are becoming young teenagers. You are on your way to becoming adults.

and for others in the hall this morning… well, they are there already.

Reader [3] For the grown ups, the signs of age are beginning to show. The grey hairs, the lines in faces, the birthdays that are best forgotten, because the numbers are getting too big and the counting is hard.

Reader [4] Today is a very important day for many people. Somewhere in our country a baby is about to be born, someone is getting ready to move house, someone else is just beginning their last day at work before retirement.

>For some people, after a long illness, today will be for them the end of their suffering.

>But for many others, today will be just another day in their lives, not very special, a day lived through without need of label.

>Maybe a day of wasted chances, of lost opportunities.

Reader [5] But maybe today is the chance for each of us to say for once,
>>yes I do have time,
>>I can listen to you,
>>I can help you,
>>I can be the friend that you need.

>Maybe sometime during today you will have the chance to use your time to help others.

>In a way today can be a bit special, a bit special for the person who shares your time and a bit special for you.

Reader [6] Many of the stories of Jesus were about people willing to give some of their time to someone else.

>On many occasions he showed, by his example, that we shouldn't rush by ignoring the needs of people about us.

>Let's listen to the story of a man hurt by the roadside.

Reader [7] The story of the Good Samaritan

[A Reading from the Gospel story or a play might follow]

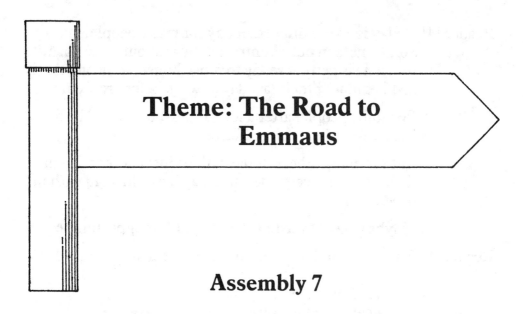

Theme: The Road to Emmaus

Assembly 7

Reader [1] Have you looked in the mirror this morning? Did it frighten you? Did you get a shock? Now you know what other people see when they look at you...

You would be very surprised if one of your friends met you in school and didn't recognise you.

Let's try something.

[Have three children covered in blankets, reveal just one hand, a foot and then part of the head. See if they can be recognised]

Reader [2] We have found just how hard it is to recognise someone just by seeing a small part of them.

One hand might look just like another hand.

Usually, it is the person's face that we recognise.

But suppose we couldn't see them. How might we recognise them?

[three different voices taped]

Reader [3] Our voices are special and just as we know our friends by their faces, so we also know them by their voices.

When we hear them speak or laugh, we know who it is.

Reader [4] What happens when we haven't seen someone for a very long time? It is easy then to make a mistake, for a person can change.

Older people begin to go grey or even lose their hair.

Haven't you heard someone say,

> 'Oh it's you,
> I didn't recognise you,
> you look different'

Reader [5] Sometimes of course people make every effort to look different. They don't want to be recognised.

So they disguise themselves, grow a beard, start wearing glasses or different clothes.

This can be done so well that they really look different, they can't be recognised.

Reader [6] On Easter Sunday morning, Jesus wasn't recognised in the Garden and later that evening, two men on the road to Emmaus didn't know who was walking with them.

Jesus was only recognised by what he did, when he broke bread and shared it with them.

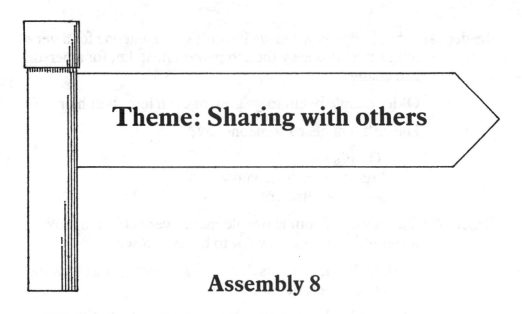

Theme: Sharing with others

Assembly 8

Reader [1] It is a chilly morning, cold and damp after rain.

    Early on a few high clouds covered the sun. Puddles still lie on the ground,

    not a day to go sunbathing.

Reader [2] It really is Autumn now, the tree colours are changing, the green of Summer has become the gold and brown of Autumn.

    As the leaves change colour they fall off the trees on to the ground.

    That is why the Americans call the Autumn 'The Fall'

Reader [3] The fields are bare now, where seeds were planted in Springtime, there is just brown earth.

    The crops have grown and the harvest has been gathered.

Reader [4] We have had our Festival of the Harvest and the money that we raised has been sent to help (-------)

    We have shared what we had with others who needed our help.

Reader [5] Jesus was once talking to a large crowd of people on a hillside. They were hungry and there didn't seem to be much food.

But there was a young boy who gave Jesus some bread and some fish.

Jesus fed the people.

How, we do not know.

Reader [0] Maybe the example of one boy giving all he had got made the others who had food share it.

Maybe.

Reader [7] As we say a prayer together this morning, remember our Festival of Harvest, especially when we use the words
   'Give us this day
   our daily bread'

Let us be very quiet and let us be very still.

PAUSE

Let us say together: "OUR FATHER..."

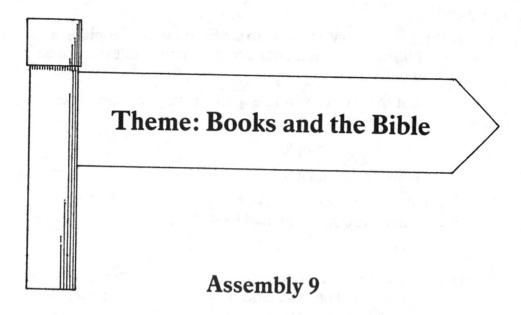

Theme: Books and the Bible

Assembly 9

[Have a large number of books at the front of the Hall, scattered on tables, chairs or the floor. Three or four children can be reading or choosing books]

Reader [1] Books, lots of them, lots and lots of books.

    Big one and small ones, thin ones and fat ones.

    More and more books.

    Some books with lots of words, some with long words, some books of pictures.

    More and more books.

Reader [2] Some books are very cheap, others very, very expensive.

    Some have hard covers like this: (------)

    Others have soft covers like this. They are called paperbacks: (------)

    Here is a song about paperback books

[Beatles: Paperback Writer - *but start a part way in… A child can be seen using a typewriter while it is playing]*

Reader [3] It's nice to know who wrote a book, to see the face and hear the voice of the person who is just a name on the cover.

I wonder how many authors we will meet?

When we pick up a book written a long time ago, we cannot see or hear the author any more.

All we have are the words on the page, the words he or she wrote, the story they told.

It can be very hard to understand if it is very old, for now, you and I are different people living in a different time.

Reader [4] We have lots of books here this morning, we are going to show you some of them.

[Children/Staff can show particular books to the group, maybe make a comment on the book, why they like it, what the story is about etc]

Reader [5] If someone writes the story of another person's life, we call it a BIOGRAPHY.

But if someone writes the story of their own life we call it an AUTOBIOGRAPHY.

I wonder if anyone here this morning will have the story of their life written in a book…

Reader [6]

[A good-sized version of the Bible should be one of the books in the collection]

This book tells the story of a people, the story of their joy and sadness, their good times and their troubles.

It tells the story of their journey to find a new land.

It tells the story of a people looking for God our Father.

We call it the Bible.

It was written a long time ago.

Reader [7] Here is one short piece from the Bible, a song written by a man called David.

Let's listen very quietly to the words.

Close your eyes, be still and listen:

[Psalm 99: Cry out with joy to the Lord all the Earth...]

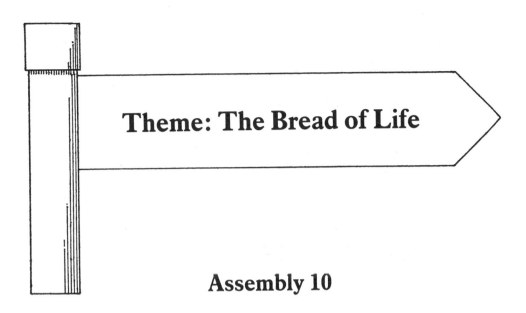

Theme: The Bread of Life

Assembly 10

[A number of food items, clothing and some bags would be useful. A child gets ready for a journey]

Reader [1] You have just seen someone begin a journey. Before such a journey, we get things ready.

We prepare our clothing, we check our transport, we find out the times of the train or the bus.

Sometimes, we prepare food to take with us on the journey, for although there might be a motorway service station or some other place where we can eat, it is often cheaper if we take our own food.

And if the journey is very long, then we shall certainly need it.

Reader [2] Even more so in years gone by. A traveller a couple of hundred years ago would certainly have taken good care to pack some food.

For without food, and even more importantly without something to drink, we very soon find ourselves tired and exhausted.

We need food and drink to keep us going.

Reader [3] On the table here this morning, you can see some bread and some drinks.

Bread, made from wheat flour was, and is, a very important food to many millions of people.

And drinks? Here is a bottle of milk and here is a bottle of lemonade. And this bottle, already opened, contains wine, a drink made from the juice of grapes.

Food and drink, energy and growth, the building blocks of life.

There are of course many other things that we eat and drink, but even with these simple foods we could keep going for a long while.

Reader [4] *[Have a large pyrex bowl of clear water on a table]*

And here is a bowl of water...

If you were in a hot country and you were given a bowl of water, which would be the most important?

A good wash? or a good drink?

Without water, there can be no life on Earth, without something to drink and food to eat, we cannot survive.

Reader [5] Jesus of Nazareth used these signs of food and drink to explain himself to the people.

On one occasion he said to his friends:

"I am the bread of life"

and another time he said:

"I am living water, he who comes to me will not be thirsty again"

He was talking to people who could not go to Tescos or Safeways, who did not have the milkman calling each morning.

These were people who grew their crops in the fields and took their water from the well.

If the crops failed to grow or the well dried up, they were in real trouble.

Reader [6] Wine was a drink well known to the Hebrew people and was often drunk with meals, especially on important occasions. The meal that Jesus shared with his friends at Passover was a very important occasion indeed, for every year the people celebrated their freedom at this meal.

On the table were pieces of bread, made without yeast, and wine.

At the end of the meal Jesus picked them up and offered them to his friends as food for their journey.

"This is myself, share it among you"

This is why, after Jesus had left his friends, whenever they gathered together they shared a meal, broke bread and passed it to each other and shared a cup of wine.

Reader [7] Christian people today still share in that meal.
They call it
'Communion', the coming together.

or sometimes they use a Greek word
'Eucharist', a meal of thanksgiving.

End with link to next? memory tile making of our holy communion this year (Summer)

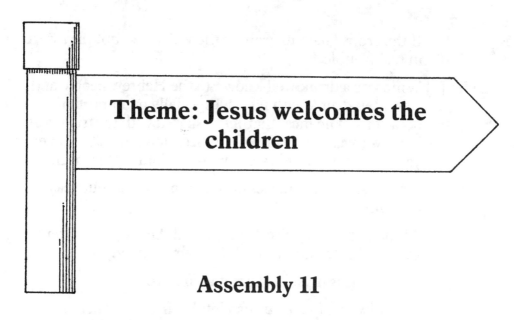

Theme: Jesus welcomes the children

Assembly 11

[A large card with the day's date written clearly]

Reader [1] I wonder if any one has had a birthday this week? Or is it someone's birthday today?

> Our birthday is very important, for it is the day we were born, the day we began to breathe air and live apart from our mother.
>
> For nine months we had grown deep within the warmth and safety of our mother, until that special day,
> > the day we were born,
> > the day we were on our own.
>
> Do you know your birth date?

Reader [2] As we grow up, we learn to walk and talk, more and more we learn to look after ourselves.

> We often spend time with our friends and when we are together we chatter and make a noise.
>
> That's the time when the grown-ups tell us that they are tired and it is time we were in bed…

Reader [3] There was one time near the end of the day, when Jesus was tired.

It had been a long, hot day and he had talked to many people.

Some children tried to get near to him, but his friends stopped them, telling the children that Jesus was tired. They were told to go away.

But Jesus called them back. He told his friends that the Kingdom of Heaven belongs to children.

He gave them his time, he welcomed them.

Reader [4] That was why, when his friends asked him about Prayer he said to them,
    'Call God your Father'

The word he used was the Hebrew word ABBA. That was short for Father, just like the words that we use, dad or daddy.

He was trying to show them that they were like children to God our Father.

Let us say together: "OUR FATHER…"

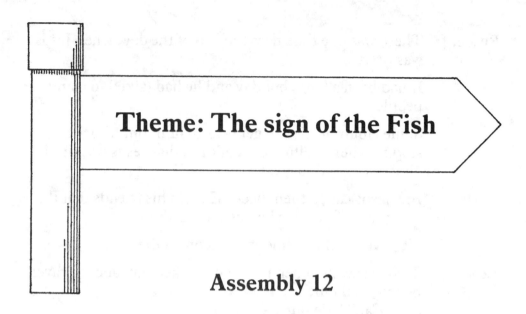

Theme: The sign of the Fish

Assembly 12

Reader [1] *[a large picture of a Road STOP sign]*

    This sign tells the car driver to STOP.

    There are many other signs that we see in the street.

    They tell car drivers what to do and where to go.

    Signs are better than words... I wonder why?

Reader [2] *[A large simple picture of a fish or other pictures of fish made by the children]*

    Here are some pictures of fish that we have drawn and painted.

    Many of the friends of Jesus were fishermen.

    They went out in boats and let down their nets to catch fish.

    They sold the fish in the market. It was very hard work.

Reader [3] The fish was also a sign for the early Christians and the simple shape is know as the IKTHUS.

    The letters of the word reminded them of Jesus. It was a sign that the person who drew it on a wall had listened to the stories of Jesus.

He was able to tell others by this sign that he was a friend of Jesus.

Reader [4] There are many other signs that Christians still use to remind them of Jesus.

One is the sign of the Cross, when a person draws a shape of the Cross on himself and says
> 'In the name of the Father
> and of the Son
> and of the Holy Spirit'

I wonder if you can find any others after our assembly?

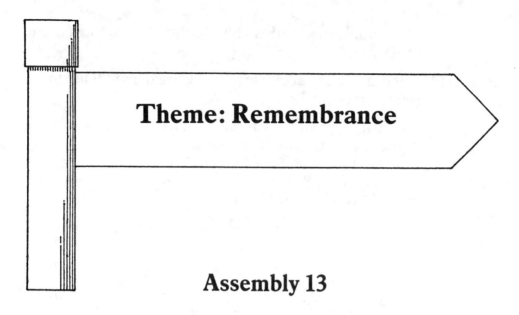

Theme: Remembrance

Assembly 13

Reader [1] November is the month of deep Autumn, the month when the leaves are finally stripped from the trees.

The month of mists and damp mornings, the month that leads to December and to Christmas, the end of the year.

Reader [2] November is also the month of memory, the month when we remember the men and women who gave their lives in time of war.

We remember them in November for it was a November day when the Great War at the start of this century finally came to an end.

It was 11 o'clock in the morning, on the 11th day of November, the 11th month in the year 1918 that the guns were finally stilled and a great silence came down over the battlefields of Europe.

Reader [3] *[picture of poppies in a field]*

Here is a field of poppies.

It is a sight that the men of the Great War remembered when they came home, the fields full of red poppies.

They took the poppy as the sign and symbol of memory. The British Legion, a group that cares for men and women from the war time who are now old or sick, makes poppies each year for us to buy.

To help them raise money,
to help us remember.

Reader [4] Shortly after that Great War, they brought back to England the body of a soldier, found on the battlefield, a man whose name was not known.

They did not know his rank or his regiment. They did not know where his home had been in England.

With great honour he was brought back to London and in the presence of the King the soldier was buried in Westminster Abbey.

If you ever go to London, there in the Abbey you will see a large brass plate on the floor.

It is the last resting place of the Unknown Soldier.

Reader [5] This Sunday we will remember again that Sunday in November 1918, when the Great War ended.

It will be remembered in London by the Queen, the Prime Minister and many other famous people.

They will lay wreaths of red poppies at the Cenotaph in Whitehall, in the centre of London.

The word Centotaph is a Greek word. It means an empty tomb.

It is a large pillar of white stone in the middle of a street called Whitehall, near to the Houses of Parliament in London.

Elsewhere, in towns and villages, there will be other occasions of memory.

Reader [6] There have been other wars since and many, many people have been killed or injured.

Let us think of them as we say our prayers this morning.
Let us remember them when we buy our Poppy.

Lord,
    As we pray for people who have died in war,
    we pray for peace.
    Teach us Lord, to love each other,
        teach us not to argue,
        teach us not to fight.

'They shall grow not old as we who are left grow old.
Age shall not weary them nor the years condemn.
At the going down of the sun and in the morning, we will remember them.' *

* *Laurence Binyon*

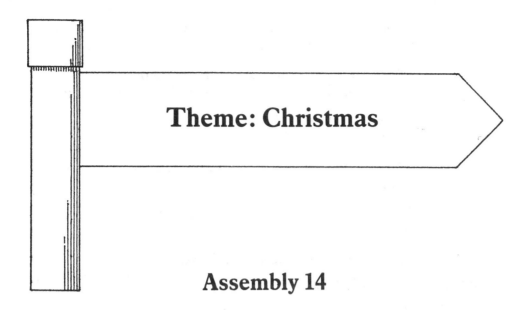

Theme: Christmas

Assembly 14

An OHP with three pictures: One of a young baby – a screen can be made from a good photograph, plus two pictures of the journey to Bethlehem and the Stable.

A piece of black sugar paper, pierced with many small holes to represent stars and a half circle for the Moon.

Start with the star screen as children come in to a darkened hall.
Music: The Carol *'O Little Town of Bethlehem.'*

Reader [1] I wonder if anyone in your family has had a baby recently?

    When you first saw it, didn't it seem small and helpless?

    Tiny fingers and no teeth. Unable to walk, maybe little hair.

    Unable to feed itself, needing milk from its mum or from a bottle.

    A new life in need of our care.

Reader [2] You see, very young humans can't help themselves.

    If it wasn't for grown-ups they couldn't survive.

    All of us were once like that, helpless.

    A baby carried in another person's arms.

    What's it like to hold a baby?

[Discussion]

Reader [3] When a baby is born we take great care to look after the mother and the new child.

>There is a new person in the family, a new name and another birthday to remember in the years to come.

>The baby has to be kept warm. It has to be fed, washed and now and then have its nappy changed.

>And day by day, it gets stronger, heavier, bigger and older.

>A lifetime's journey has begun. It was the same for all of us.

>Once upon a time we were all like that.

[Change OHP from baby to the journey slide]

Reader [4] The Child of Mary, the baby boy that she called Jesus, was born after a long journey.

>Mary had been taken by her husband Joseph from their village, a place called Nazareth, to the city of Bethlehem.

>A difficult and dangerous journey. And when they got there, they found everywhere was full.

>There were so many people in the town that there was no where for them to sleep.

>They got shelter for the night in the yard at the back of the hotel.

>There, with the animals, they settled down for the night.

[OHP of the Stable scene]

Reader [5] During that night, Mary's baby was born. A baby boy, just as helpless as we were, a child needing love and care, a child who had to be fed and clothed.

>Mary called her baby Jesus.

>And that is the story of Christmas, the story of a baby born in a Stable.

>Child, where have you come from?

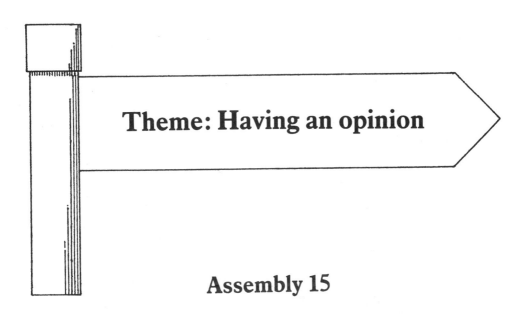

Theme: Having an opinion

Assembly 15

A chair and table, a newspaper, an old coat and hat. Tape of 'Nowhere Man' – The Beatles.

Reader [1] Good morning, everyone, and how are you this morning?

[Tape: Nowhere Man: a child dressed in an old coat and a hat walks in, settles down in the armchair and reads the newspaper. Fade out tape]

Reader [0] Let's ask the Nowhere Man a few questions.

Reader [2] What do you think of [.........]?

[The answers can be written on the inside of the Newspaper the Nowhere Man is reading.]

[Nowhere man]: Well, er... no... er... not much... really.
         I really don't... er know.

Reader [2] What did you think of the news yesterday?

[Nowhere man]: well, I, um... don't understand it.
         You see... never take much... um
         interest... in the news.

Reader [2] What are you doing this Summer?

[Nowhere man]: Well, um... I don't have any... um plans not yet anyway... Don't really... know... what's happening... you see...

[The Nowhere Man goes back to reading his newspaper, the questioner turns away, throwing up his hands in despair.]

Reader [3] Our Nowhere Man is a lively character, isn't he? Really bouncy, full of energy. A 'get up and go man' in every sense. Strong views, firm opinions, really knows where he is going, doesn't he?

PAUSE...

No, not really. He didn't come over that way at all, did he? He didn't have a point of view, he didn't know where he was going at all, did he?

[The Nowhere Man tilts his hat over his eyes and goes to sleep, taking no further part.]

Reader [4] When we say that someone is entitled to their point of view, it doesn't mean that they will always be 'right' or that we will have to agree with them.

But we must respect their opinions, even if we totally disagree with them.

Reader [5] Our point of view gets formed in many ways.

We talk to and listen to our friends.

We hear our parents talking, we listen to our teachers,

we watch television, listen to records and tapes and the radio.

We read books, comics and newspapers, go to the pictures.

All these things help to form our point of view.

They help us to avoid being like the Nowhere Man...

'Who doesn't have a point of view, who doesn't know where he is going to. Isn't he a bit like you and me?'

Maybe, but as we grow up we must try to be better than that.

Reader [6] The older we get, the more choices we have to make.

And we can only make choices if, first, we have really thought about the problem.

We will find all sorts of pressures on us to act in a certain way,

or to hold certain opinions

or to go about with certain people.

In the end, we have to decide for ourselves.

But in making that decision, we cannot ignore other people.

We have to live on Earth with other people. We have to get on with them.

In trying not to be a Nowhere Person we have our own views and opinions.

We want to be respected by others and in return we must learn to respect them.

Reader [7] *[The text of the song might be read here]*

Reader [8] Our hymn this morning tells the story of an argument,

the forming of an opinion.

It tells the story of Judas and Mary, arguing over what to do with a pot of oil...

of Judas, who wanted to sell it and then to give the money to the poor...,

of Mary, who wanted to show Jesus a sign of her love and anointed his feet.

It shows that often the most obvious solution to a problem is not always the best solution,

that it is worth taking time to talk out a problem, before we charge off and act in haste.

[Hymn Judas and Mary – *Sydney Carter]*

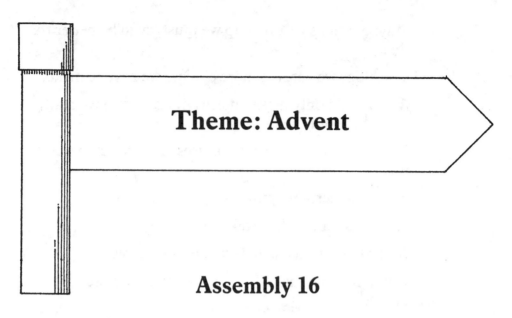

Theme: Advent

Assembly 16

[Start with a darkened hall, maybe two or three candles alight and some quiet music, set an atmosphere of stillness as the children arrive]

Reader [1] A world without electricity would now seen very strange to us.

    Homes without light, streets in darkness, cities wrapped in gloom.

    And yet, it is not that long ago when life WAS like that.

    And the only light after the Sun had set was from the fire at home and from candles.

    It must have been a very different world indeed

Reader [2] Over a period of time, things change.

    The world that we live in now may seem just as strange and different to the people who will live in the future.

    They will look back and wonder at the way we live and the things we have to put up with.

    'Time will say nothing, but I told you so' *

Reader [3] We look forward to things changing, to new things coming and old ways put aside.

We look forward to better things, always expecting that life will improve, that something else is just around the corner.

We look forward to parties, to birthdays and holidays and friends coming to our home.

Memories are important but they soon become part of our history story.

We are excited and hopeful about the future and what is still to come.

Reader [4] For the Hebrew people in Israel, this was true as well.

Over many hundreds of years, they looked forward to the promise of the Lord, the promise that someone would come, someone to help them,
    to guide them,
    to save them.

They called him the MESSIAH or sometimes the CHRIST.

He was to be the light of their world, He was to bring them a new start, a fresh beginning.

His Advent, His Coming, was their dream.

Reader [5] And now again, it is the time of ADVENT, a small word that just means the COMING.

We are looking forward again to the time we call Christmas, looking forward to the coming of the Christ Child,

The baby of Bethlehem, Jesus.

[An Advent reading or a story about Christmas and an Advent hymn can finish this Assembly].

★ *W H Auden*

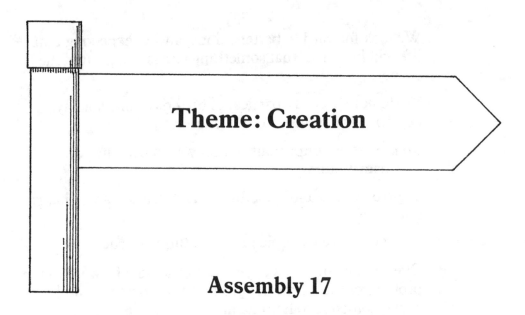

Theme: Creation

Assembly 17

[A large picture of the Earth from space, either a painting or an OHP screen. Winter scenes painted by the children, bare twigs in a pot]

Reader [1] A dark and dreary morning, wet and misty, and cold.

    It is the very depths of Winter.

    The trees are bare, nothing seems to be growing, there is a stillness about the place,

    almost a death of the earth.

Reader [2] With the coming of Spring in a few weeks time, things that looked dead will again burst into life.

    Newness will come from the dark soil, plants will begin to grow, leaves come back to the trees.

    The cycle of live on our planet Earth will begin again.

[An old piece of tree root, found by children on a beach, was the centre piece of this Assembly.]

Reader [3] This piece of wood will never grow again.

    It is the remains of a tree found many years ago on a beach.

    It was full of sand and covered in seaweed.

Where had it come from?

Had it been washed away from the shore line as tides ebbed and flowed?

Or had it been brought by that same tide from a distant shore line?

We will never know.

All that is left is a hollow shell, the dead remains of something that once grew, that once gave shelter.

[A picture of Stonehenge or some other stone circle]

Reader [4] Things that are old intrigue us.

> We wonder,
>> where did they come from?
>> who made them?
>> what were they used for?
>
> We try to imagine the whole scene, to work out the details from the few clues that remain.
>
>> Standing stones,
>
> Why? What were they for? How did they get there? What stories could they tell?

Reader [5] But the very Earth we live on is much, much older than the bits and pieces we find.

> Maybe as old as four thousand million years...
>
> A number so big it is hard to imagine it.
>
> It is a long, long time ago.

Reader [6] The Hebrew people tried to imagine what it was like in that very early time, the time when the Earth was made.

> When they wrote about it, they tried to show that whatever happened it was God who was the source of the energy and life that began then.
>
> Let's listen to a short passage from the very start of the Book of Genesis.

The word GENESIS means BIRTH, the Beginning, the start of things.

[The first few verses of Genesis can be read in a suitable translation. A slide of the Earth rise over the Moon, and mention of the first Apollo Moon Mission, Christmas 68, when this narrative was read from Space, can also be made.]

Hymn: The Lord of the Dance: *Sydney Carter*
(Celebration Hymnal no. 131)

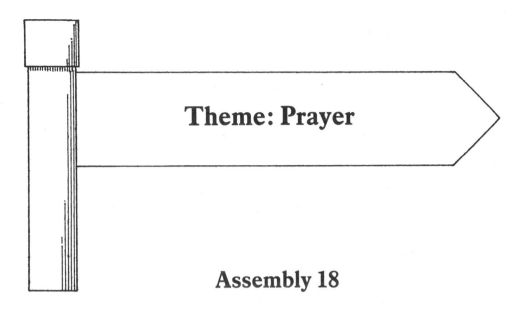

Theme: Prayer

Assembly 18

[Tape: 'You just call on my name'*: Carole King]*

Reader [1] 'You just call on my name,
    and you know where ever I am,
    I'll come running to see you again.

    Winter, Spring, Summer or Fall,
    all you have to do is call,
    and I'll be there,
    yes I will, I'll be there.
    You've got a friend'

    You have just heard that song being sung as you came into the hall this morning.

    Now that we are all sitting down, let's listen to some of it again, this time very quietly, listening to the words.

[Replay part of the Tape]

Reader [2] If we are in trouble we expect someone to help us.

    Mum or dad, a brother or a sister, grandma or a friend.

    To have no one to turn to,
        no one to share your troubles,
        no one to give a few moments

- that would indeed be lonely.

We need each other.

Someone else, someone who will listen to our story,

Someone who will give some time,
   Give us the chance to share.

Reader [3] But it is not just the troubles that we need to share.

There are many other things, times of great joy, happy events that are made even better by being shared with others.

These times, too, are part of our story, made so much better by being shared.

Reader [4] We expect a bit of attention,
   a bit of time,
something set aside,
   just for us.

We wouldn't be very impressed with a friend who said
   she did really want to share in our story,

but insisted on watching EastEnders while we told her the detail.

When we finished, we would be left wondering…

'Well, just how much did she hear?
   Does she really care?
   Was it worth the telling…?

I don't think I'll bother next time.'

We like to know that others listen to us.

It might remind each one of us that we too should listen when they are telling us something.

Reader [5] All over Planet Earth, our common home,

People of all ages, different colours and races, different backgrounds,
   share one obvious thing,

they are all human beings.

They eat and breath, experience joy and sorrow, and at the end of the day
fall asleep just as we do.

And many of them spend some time each day telling their story to God our Father.

They call it Prayer.

Sometimes that Prayer is said alone, in the quietness of a room.

At other times it is said in a great crowd of people, together praising God, together sharing with each other and with Him.

Reader [6] Let's listen for a few moments to a group of people who are praying through song.

Let's listen very quietly, and even if we can't hear the exact words they are singing, maybe we can appreciate something of the depth of their prayer.

[Tape of Music from Taizé.
Fade out the tape and leave a few moments of stillness and complete silence.]

Reader [1] Now let's add our Morning Prayer to God our Father as we say together:

"OUR FATHER..."

[The Assembly can end with a hymn if required, or part of the Taizé tape played on]

Theme: Good News

Assembly 19

[This Assembly should be prefaced with an audio tape recording of a Morning News Bulletin or a video recording of Breakfast Television News for that morning]

Reader [1] We have just listened to [seen] the news this morning.

It has told us of the recent events in our own country and elsewhere on the earth.

Every hour of the day, we can hear the latest News.

Or if we have Teletext we can search the pages for the latest News.

[If teletext is available, this could be called up in front of the children by one of the readers]

Reader [2] So often, the News tells of sad events.

We hear of a plane crash
   or an explosion in a city.

We hear of an accident in a mine
   or the death of a famous person.

We hear stories of dishonesty,
   stories of selfishness,
   and stories of greed.

You wonder sometimes, just why we bother to turn it on.

Reader [3] Wouldn't it make a change if, just for once, we could hear a GOOD NEWS News Bulletin.

It might sound something like this:

'Good morning everyone,
here is the news for today... [date]'

Reader [4] This morning it was reported that all aircraft leaving London Heathrow landed safely.

Last night, there were no explosions in Belfast.

Lloyds Bank have told us that throughout yesterday, all their branches remained open and no one tried to rob them of money.

The men at the local Fire Station spent an idle day, with no fires and no 999 calls to answer.

The weather forecast for today is that we will all be having some weather, most of it just what we need.

The next Good News Bulletin will be at 10 o'clock. Have a nice day.

Reader [3] The trouble is that after a short while no one would bother listening to the News.

The interesting things, the exciting things, the dramatic things
     so very often involve misfortune.

it's the Big Story, the event that is different, that makes the News.

Reader [4] The Four Gospels, written by Matthew, Mark, Luke and John, tell us the story of the life of Jesus.

The word GOSPEL means GOOD NEWS.

The stories they tell, the events they describe, the people they mention, all in the end are Good News for us.

For the Gospels tell us the story of God's love and concern for all of us. It is the story that shows all of us the way to God our Father.

It is indeed Good News.

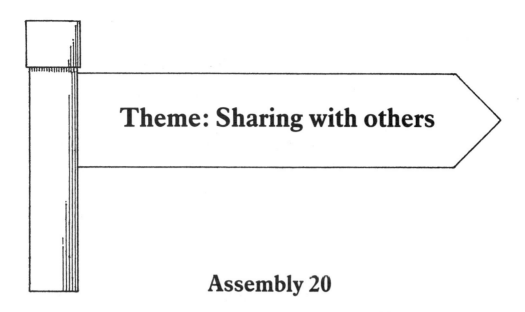

Theme: Sharing with others

Assembly 20

[Some simple items of food, some milk, bread and cakes. Laid out on a table, ready to eat. Plates and cups. Two visitors are required]

Reader [1] If someone stopped you in the street, shook you by the hand and with a smile, said to you:

> "You are very greedy, selfish and thoughtless"

would you be pleased?

Would you walk away from that person, saying to yourself...

> I am pleased I met him this morning.

> He has really made me feel great,
> what a smashing person I must be.

> I hope he tells his friends all about me.
> Maybe they will come and shake my
> hand as well
> and say a big thank you'

Somehow, I don't think so.

Reader [2] *[Wait for the arrival of the two visitors]*

    Good morning to you both. Nice to see you.

    You look fit and well this bright, cheerful morning.

    Everything alright?

    Of course it is, sit down and join us. I am sure you would like to listen to the rest of our Assembly this morning.

    When you're sitting comfortably, we'll continue.

Reader [3] How about giving one of our visitors some breakfast?

    Nothing too extravagant, just a few rolls and some other bits and pieces.

    Can't have our guests saying we aren't generous to them, can we?

[Wait while the food is offered to one of the visitors. Every time the other visitor tries to get near the table he is pushed away, while a great fuss is made of the one who is being fed.]

    That's it, you enjoy yourself.

    Our Breakfast Bar is known all over town.

    When you leave, tell your friends what a grand time you had here.

    Aren't we generous?

[Before they leave, give the one who has been fed some extra clothing. Leave the other visitor with nothing, even though he asks for something]

Reader [4] *[The two visitors gather up their belongings and leave. One licks his lips, satisfied, the other obviously upset as he has had nothing.]*

    But will both of them tell the same story?

    Will they BOTH say how warm they were, and how comfortable we made them? and how well we fed them?

    Here is the story of a large gathering of people who came together on a hillside to listen to Jesus of Nazareth.

They were hungry and they didn't have a local supermarket where why could buy the food they needed.

Listen quietly.

[Read from a suitable text the story of the Feeding of the Five Thousand. Talk about the need to share.]

Theme: Forgiveness

Assembly 21

[Some pieces of burnt wood, some large nails. Pictures of bombed buildings. Tape recording of a siren.]

Reader [1] *[Just before the Reader starts to read, play the tape of an air raid siren, and/or sound of explosions.]*

In the Midlands of our country is the city of Coventry.

One night in 1940, a night in November, the city suffered a terrible air raid.

One result of that air raid was the destruction of the great Cathedral in the city:
  it was reduced to ruins.

the roof was completely destroyed and all the furnishings inside were burnt.

By morning, the people of the city were left with a smoking pile of timbers and stones.

Only the very outer walls were left standing.

Reader [2] Many other buildings were destroyed and many people lost their lives.

But the loss of the Cathedral that stood at the heart of the city hurt the people.

It had been there since the 14th century, and now it was gone.

[PAUSE]

Or was it?

Reader [3] A few days after the bombing, two rough pieces of charred oak from the roof of the Cathedral, one 12 foot long, the other 8 foot in length, were tied together with wire and fixed in an old dustbin filled with sand.

This charred wooden Cross was later to become famous all over the world.

Reader [4] When the roof beams burnt, many hundreds of nails were found scattered across the floor.

They were collected from the ruins and later by bending and twisting the metal, they were used to make many much smaller Crosses.

After the war was over, they were presented to many centres throughout the world
> as a sign of peace,
> a sign of forgiveness.

And the great charred Cross was stood in the shell of the ancient Cathedral, in front of words carved in the stone:

FATHER, FORGIVE

Reader [5] Since those days and the end of that terrible War, a new Cathedral has been built, not on the site of the old one, but alongside it.

You can still walk through the remains of the old building, and see on the wall those words,

FATHER FORGIVE.

It has become a centre for people to try to understand each other, a place to forgive.

It is a sign that the Christian Churches should care for each other.

Reader [6] Jesus told his friends:

> "I pray that you may be one
> as the Father and I are one,
> that you may be one in us."

Remember those words of forgiveness from Coventry as we say together:

"OUR FATHER..."

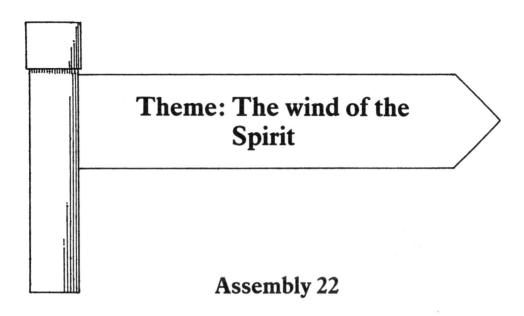

Theme: The wind of the Spirit

Assembly 22

[A sound effects recording of wind in a storm.]

Reader [1] When the wind blows, the trees sway and wave in the sky.

When the wind blows, the leaves on the ground fly into the air.

When the wind blows, papers are tossed. When the wind blows.

Reader [2] When the wind blows, you can feel it on your face.

We can feel it blowing our hair, we can feel it blowing into our clothes.

It is hard to walk against the wind, especially when you are small.

Reader [3] When the wind blows, it makes a great noise,

we can hear it in the trees, doors bang and windows rattle.

Dustbins clatter, when the wind blows.

Reader [4] When the wind blows at night time, we can lie in bed and listen to it.

It is strong and powerful.

We listen to that wind outside our bedroom window.

If it is raining, the wind blows the rain onto our window.

It is noisy when the wind blows.

Reader [5] When the wind gets really strong, we call it a gale.

And a wind in a gale can cause things to break.

Windows and chimney pots, doors and trees and slates from the roof of a house.

When the wind blows.

Reader [6] In the days after Easter time, the friends of Jesus were together in a room of a house in Jerusalem.

We are told that they heard a rushing noise, like a great wind.

And it was at this time that the Spirit came to them.

They stopped being frightened and went outside to talk to the people about Jesus of Nazareth.

Like a strong wind, the Spirit gave them the courage to tell the story of Jesus.

Like a strong wind, their words swept through the land and people listened.

Reader [7] When we breathe we make a very small wind blow: for us, that wind is the breath of life. Without it we couldn't live.

[PAUSE]

'Come Holy Spirit, Come
fill the hearts of your people,
let your wind kindle in us
the fire of your love.
From the Spirit of God, give us life.'

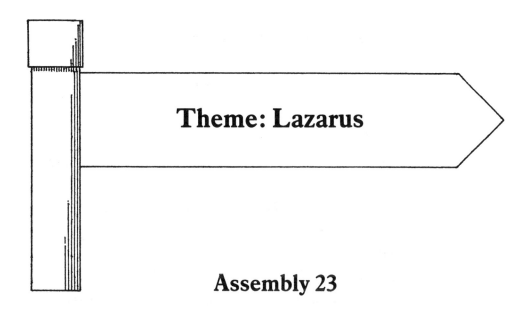

Theme: Lazarus

Assembly 23

Reader [1] The Gospel stories tell us many things about Jesus of Nazareth.

We hear about his friends and the journeys they made together.

We hear about the people they met and spoke to. We hear about the crowds that gathered round him, and the many questions that they asked.

At the end of the day there must have been many occasions when he was exhausted, when he wanted some peace and quiet.

Away from the crowds and the dusty roads.

When, just like us, he wanted to put his feet up and rest.

Reader [2] Jesus and his friends use to go to the village called Bethany, just outside the great city of Jerusalem.

There, they often went to the house of two sisters, Martha and Mary.

In their house, there was rest and relaxation.

Martha and Mary knew Jesus and his friends very well.

Martha and Mary also had a brother, a man called Lazarus.

He must have often shared a meal at the same table.

Jesus and his friends, with Martha and Mary and their brother Lazarus.

Reader [3] One day, news came to Jesus and his friends that Lazarus was ill.

They were on the far side of the River Jordan at the time.

In fact, the message they received made it clear that Lazarus was likely to die.

So they began to make their way to Bethany, to the house of Martha and Mary, so that they could be with them.

[PAUSE: some music to indicate a journey]

But they did not arrive in time, for when they got there, they found that Lazarus was already dead.

In fact he had already been buried in a rock tomb and the great stone rolled across to cover the entrance.

Reader [4] And Jesus, who loved this man, cried with them and was sad.

He shared in the grief of the sisters and the whole village.

He asked them to show him where Lazarus had been buried.

When they took him to the place, Jesus surprised them all.

He called out to Lazarus.

To everyone's amazement, Lazarus came out to them. He was alive after all.

Reader [5] The word spread through the village very quickly, that Jesus had somehow brought Lazarus back to them, and that he had returned to his sisters, to Martha and Mary.

No one could understand it, they were puzzled and some of them were afraid.

Others came to listen to his words more carefully. They were curious about this man and the stories that they had heard.

Lazarus, the man Jesus loved, was alive. He was back at his home with Martha and Mary, and the people could see him.

Jesus had shown them the love of God our Father.

And some of the people began to listen to him more carefully.

Reader [6] The story of Lazarus is our story too.

It is the story of the love that God our Father has for each one of us.

It is the story of the promise that God made to his people.

It is the story of the promise of life.

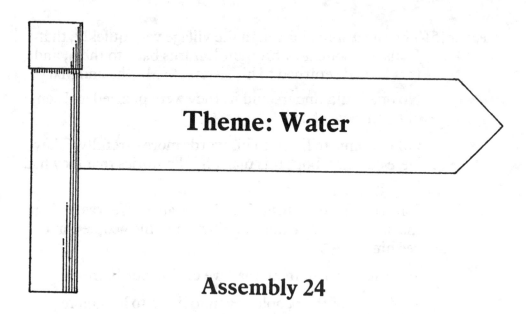

Theme: Water

Assembly 24

[A large bowl or jug of water, some soap, a towel and a beaker]

Reader [1] Did you wash this morning?

    Did you have a drink?

    Did you flush the toilet?

    I wonder how much water you used – and it's still early in the day.

    By the end of the day all of us will have used lots of water.

[Pour some water in to the bowl, let a child wash their hands with soap and water. Pour some water in to the beaker, offer a child a drink.]

Reader [2] When the Summer is hot and long, when very little rain falls, we call it a drought.

    Then we have to be careful how much water we use.

    If you had very little water and it was very hot,
        would you wash with it
        or would you drink it?

Reader [3] We need water to live.

> You can go many days without food.
>
> But you can't survive for long without drinks. Water keeps us alive.
>
> We like to keep ourselves clean, but if there is a choice,
>
> then we will go dirty and use the water to drink.

Reader [4] John, who was a cousin of Jesus, met him one day by the River Jordan.

> John poured water from the river over the head of Jesus, as a sign of life.
>
> This is why John is called the Baptist.
>
> It was the start of the time when Jesus began to teach the people about God our Father.

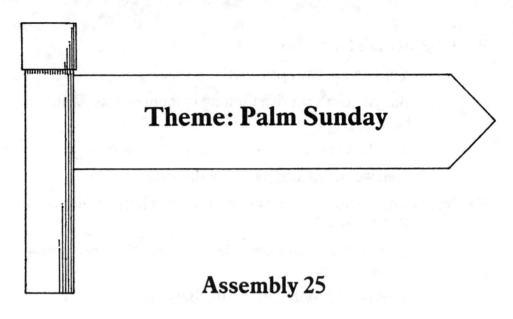

Theme: Palm Sunday

Assembly 25

Reader [1] It was getting near to the time of the great feast of Passover.

Every year the Hebrew people celebrated their freedom at the time they called Passover.

The city of Jerusalem could be crowded with people at this time of the year.

For many weeks, there had been gossip about Jesus and his friends:

"Would they dare come in to the City at Passover?"

If they did, then Jesus risked being arrested.

He had upset too many people, especially some of the religious leaders.

Reader [2] A few days before the Passover, when the streets were full, and the shops open, the decision was made.

Over the hills a group of people could be seen approaching the city gates.

As they got nearer, the word began to be passed round amongst the crowd:

> "He's coming!"
>
> "The man from Nazareth is on his way"
>
> "Jesus the Teacher is coming after all"
>
> "What's going to happen now?"

Reader [3] As he entered the city, the people were surprised to find that he was riding a donkey.

> A small creature, often used to carry baggage, by no means a grand animal.
>
> Jesus would have found it difficult to keep his feet off the ground.
>
> In fact, it must have looked rather funny really.

Reader [4] With him were the group of men who had been his friends for nearly three years.

> There must have been some women in the group, possible Martha and Mary, the friends he had been staying with in Bethany.
>
> Maybe his own Mother, Mary,
>
> was with them, we don't know.
>
> As they came through the narrow streets together, the people began shouting and calling out to him:
>
>> "Hosanna!
>>
>> Welcome, Son of David,
>>
>> welcome to Jerusalem!
>>
>> We're pleased to see you"

Reader [5] The people climbed the palm trees nearby and stripped the long leaves.

> They laid them on the ground in front of the donkey as a sign of welcome for Jesus.

Reader [6] Everyone was very happy and please to see Jesus. He had come after all.

> But behind all the shouts of joy and cheering, there must have been a hint of trouble, the worry that things could go wrong.
>
> It couldn't have been long before the Chief Priest and other religious leaders heard that he had arrived.
>
> But for the moment though, it was all shouts of happiness and welcome.
>
> The Lord had come to his people and they welcomed him at Passover.

[Tape of Hosanna *from* Jesus Christ Superstar]